Corporate Acquisitions and Mergers in Belgium

Corporate Acquisitions and Mergers in Belgium

Jean-Michel Detry

DLA Piper

This book was originally published as a chapter in Corporate Acquisitions and Mergers.

General Editor: Peter Begg

Wolters Kluwer

Published by:
Kluwer Law International B.V.
PO Box 316
2400 AH Alphen aan den Rijn
The Netherlands
Website: www.wolterskluwerlr.com

Sold and distributed in North, Central and South America by:
Wolters Kluwer Legal & Regulatory U.S.
7201 McKinney Circle
Frederick, MD 21704
United States of America
Email: customer.service@wolterskluwer.com

Sold and distributed in all other countries by:
Quadrant
Rockwood House
Haywards Heath
West Sussex
RH16 3DH
United Kingdom
Email: international-customerservice@wolterskluwer.com

Printed on acid-free paper

ISBN 978-90-411-8991-2

This title is available on www.wolterskluwerlr.com

Printed and Bound by CPI Group (UK) Ltd, Croydon, CR0 4YY.

DLA Piper

DLA Piper is one of the world's largest law firms, with offices across Asia Pacific, Africa, Europe, the Middle East and the Americas. With a direct presence in over thirty countries and relationship firms in jurisdictions where the firm does not have its own offices, DLA Piper represents clients and helps them with their legal needs wherever they do business. DLA Piper's global footprint enables its teams to work cross-border and to project manage complex multi-jurisdictional transactions, while preserving a single point of contact approach.

In Belgium, DLA Piper operates from two offices, in Brussels and in Antwerp. Recognized among Belgian leading law firms with over 100 lawyers, DLA Piper advises national and international companies, national governments and institutions across all areas of business law and industry sectors.

Author

Jean-Michel Detry is a member of the Brussels and of the Luxembourg Bars. His main areas of expertise include corporate law, mergers and acquisitions and commercial law. He also has expertise in corporate finance.

In the area of corporate and M&A, Jean-Michel Detry assists clients in connection with corporate and group restructuring, acquisitions and takeovers of privately held or publicly listed companies and private equity transactions. This includes the setting up of holding and finance companies, national and cross-border mergers, pre-acquisition legal audits, negotiation of share purchase agreements or asset deals, joint venture and shareholders' agreements, corporate compliance work as well as all work related to agreements, corporate reorganization and private equity.

Jean-Michel Detry is also a well-known litigator, handling acquisition related litigation, shareholders disputes, protection of minority shareholders, directors' liability cases and post-acquisition disputes. In this respect, he represents clients in court and acts as counsel to parties or as arbitrator in domestic and international arbitration cases.

Acknowledgements

The author wishes to express special thanks to the following lawyers in the Brussels office of DLA Piper for their assistance in connection with the updating of this chapter: Virginie Lescot for her assistance in connection the update of the corporate law sections, Gregory Komlosi and Tom Schepens, for their assistance in connection with the update of the tax section, Daniel Colgan and Bram Vereecken for their assistance in connection with the update of the competition law section and Eddy Lievens and Pierre Dion for their assistance in connection with the update of the labour law section.

Contents

INTRODUCTION

[01] Since 2000, company law has undergone a large number of changes in Belgium, coupled with some very important developments.

[02] The first major change was brought in by the Act of 7 May 1999, introducing the Companies Code, and its implementing Royal Decree of 30 January 2001. The new Companies Code replaced the Commercial Companies Acts, which were consolidated on 30 November 1935. Since it came into force on 6 February 2001, the Code has already undergone a number of wide-sweeping changes. For instance, the Act of 2 August 2002 and the Act of 2 May 2007 on the publicity of major holdings of issuers whose shares are admitted to trading on a regulated market and introducing miscellaneous provisions amended the company law provisions on the management and control of private companies as well as companies having made a public call to investor.

[03] Similarly, the Act of 17 December 2008, which chiefly introduced audit committees for listed companies and financial institutions, also amended a number of Companies Code provisions to bolster the quality of financial information provided to the general public.

[04] The Act of 2 August 2002 on regulation of the financial sector and financial services sets forth a range of duties of information incumbent on issuers of financial instruments and sets down rules on insider trading. The act also contains provisions dealing with the powers of the Financial Services and Markets Authority (the FSMA), formerly the Banking, Finance and Insurance Commission (the CBFA).

[05] As far as takeover bids are concerned, the entire domain is governed by the Act of 1 April 2007, together with its implementing Royal Decree of 27 April 2007, which transposes Directive 2004/25/EC.

[06] The legal and fiscal regime for cross-border mergers has also seen a number of significant developments. On the one hand, section 77 of the Financial Arrangements (Miscellaneous Provisions) Act of 8 June 2008 transposes the terms of Directive 2005/56/EC of 26 October 2005 on cross-border mergers of limited liability companies into Belgian law. On the other hand, the Act of 11 December 2008 transposing the European Directive of 17 February 2005 has introduced new tax rules on cross-border reorganizations.

[07] Recently, the economic legislation has been thoroughly reformed and is now embodied in the Code of Economic Law (CEL) dated 29 March 2013.

THE REGULATORY FRAMEWORK

Act of 2 March 1989 on the Disclosure of Shareholdings in Listed Companies and on Take-Over Bids, Implemented by the Royal Decrees of 10 May 1989 and 8 November 1989

[08] The Act of 2 March 1989 on the disclosure of major share interests in companies listed in Belgium. The first chapter of the Act, amended by the Act of 18 July 1991 and the Act of 2 August 2002, related to the disclosure of share interests. A Royal Decree implementing the first chapter of this Act was promulgated on 10 May 1989.

[09] Before being repealed by the Royal Decree of 27 April 2007, this Act also contained the second chapter on takeover bids and changes in controlling interests in companies that make, or have made, public offers to investors. The Royal Decree of 8 November 1989 implementing the second chapter of this act was also repealed by the Royal Decree of 27 April 2007.

Act of 6 August 1993 on the Fiscal Aspects of Mergers and Divisions

[10] The fiscal aspects of mergers and acquisitions were basically regulated by the Act of 22 December 1989. This act was amended by the Act of 6 August 1993, which came into force on the same date as the Act of 29 June 1993, i.e., 1 October 1993. The fiscal aspects of acquisitions and mergers are discussed below.

Act of 6 April 1995 on the Status and Control of Investment Undertakings and on Investment Intermediaries and Advisers

[11] This act contains provisions governing investment undertakings and their control, investment intermediaries and advisers. It no longer contains provisions governing secondary markets, stock exchanges or their control.

Act of 7 May 1999 (Companies Code)

[12] The Act of 7 May 1999, named the Companies Code, constitutes a general codification of most of the statutory provisions applicable to companies, including economic interest groupings and agricultural companies. The Companies Code combines provisions of civil law, commercial law and accounting law. It came into force on 6 February 2001. The Companies Code replaces the Consolidated Commercial Companies Acts, which formerly governed commercial companies.

Act of 2 August 2002 on Supervision of the Financial Sector and Financial Services

[13] This act regulates secondary markets for financial instruments and their control. It contains provisions governing financial markets as well as transactions relating to financial instruments. In this regard, the act lays down the various duties of information incumbent on an issuer of financial instruments and sets out the new rules on insider trading.

[14] This act also contains the provisions relating to the establishment of the Belgian regulator, the Financial Services and Market Authority ('FSMA'), its status and its powers.

Act of 2 August 2002 Amending the Companies Code and the Act of 2 March 1989 on the Disclosure of Shareholdings in Listed Companies and Takeover Bids

[15] This act made important amendments to company law relating to the management and control of private companies as well as companies having made a public calls to investors. According to corporate governance principles, the main goal pursued by this act was to improve propriety in the operation of companies with regard to their management and investors.

Act of 16 June 2006 on Public Offers of Investment Securities and the Admission of Investment Securities for Trading on Regulated Markets

[16] This act was intended *inter alia* to incorporate into Belgian law the provisions of two European directives: (a) the Directive of 4 November 2003 on the prospectus to be published when securities are offered to the public or admitted to trading; (b) the Directive of 9 March 2005 organizing new committees with regards to financial services.

Takeover Bids Act of 1 April 2007 and Its Royal Decrees of 27 April 2007 on Public Share Purchase and Takeover Bids

[17] The entire rules governing takeover bids are now set down in the Takeover Bids Act of 1 April 2007, the Royal Decree of 27 April 2007 on public share purchase offers and the Royal Decree of 27 April 2007 on takeover bids. The Act is a transposition of Directive 2004/25/EC of 21 April 2004 on takeover bids and is more generally intended to modernize the rules governing all public share purchase bids. The Takeover Bids Act and its two implementing royal decrees thus incorporate, with minor alterations, the majority of the provisions dealing with takeover procedures that were hitherto contained in Chapter II of the Act of 2 March 1989 and in the Royal Decree of 8 November 1989 on takeover bids and changes in the control of companies together with the public disclosure provisions previously contained in the Act of 22 April 2003.

The Royal Decree of 14 November 2007 on the Obligations on Issuers of Financial Instruments Admitted for Trading on a Belgian Regulated Market

[18] This Royal Decree lays down a general obligation incumbent on any financial issuer admitted to a market regulated in Belgium to communicate to the general public any information necessary for the transparency, integrity and proper functioning of the market. Certain specific obligations are also laid down in relation to periodic and occasional information requiring to be disclosed.

Act of 17 December 2008, in Particular Instituting Audit Committees in Listed Companies and Financial Undertakings

[19] This Act amends certain sections of the Companies Code to bolster the quality of financial information issued and is aimed at streamlining corporate management. In particular, the Act transposes certain provisions of Directive 2006/43/EC.

Finance (Miscellaneous Provisions) Act of 8 June 2008 (Official Gazette, 16 June 2008)

[20] Section 77 of the Act transposes into Belgian law the provisions of Directive 2005/56/EC of 26 October 2005 on cross-border mergers of limited liability companies. These rules are now contained in the new title VI bis ('*Specific rules on cross-border mergers and equivalent transactions*') of book XI ('Corporate reorganisations').

Act of 11 December 2008 Transposing the European Directive of 17 February 2005

[21] This Act introduced the new tax rules on cross-border reorganizations. It transposed Directive 90/434/EEC of 23 July 1990 on the common system of taxation applicable to mergers, divisions, transfers of assets and exchanges of shares concerning companies of different Member States.

The 2009 Belgian Code on Corporate Governance

[22] In 2004 the Corporate Governance Committee published the Belgian Code on Corporate Governance for listed companies. This document refers to the latest version of the redrafted Code dated 12 March 2009.

The Code of Economic Law of 29 March 2013

[23] Between 2010 and 2014, the economic legislation has been thoroughly reformed. The reformed economic legislation is now embodied in the CEL dated 29 March 2013. This code replaces, amongst others, the Act on market practices and consumer protection of 2010.

SPECIFIC LEGAL PROVISIONS

Transfer of Shares and the Legal Monopoly of Banks and Registered Brokers

[24] With a few exceptions, the Act of 2 August 2002 on the supervision of the financial sector and financial services maintains the traditional principle that all transactions involving listed securities have to be effected on the stock market. In this respect, section 24 of this act lists exceptions to the obligation on investors to go through the stock market when carrying out transactions involving financial instruments listed on a stock exchange and issued by Belgian establishments and undertakings. This principle does not apply to:

(a) occasional transactions between private individuals;
(b) the assignment of financial instruments conferring at least 10% of the voting rights of the issuing company or entity;
(c) assignments of financial instruments conferring voting rights between closely linked companies;
(d) transactions between different departments of the same collective investment undertaking as referred to in Book III of the Act of 4 December 1990 on financial transactions and financial markets.

[25] Upon the recommendation of the FSMA, the King may exclude professional investors from the scope of paragraph 1, under such conditions and limits as he may determine.

Notification of Major Transfers

[26] We would point out that operations in which it is intended to dispose of one-third or more of the share capital of an undertaking whose business is located in Belgium and whose equity amounts to EUR2 500 000 or more must first be notified to the Minister for Economic Affairs, the Minister of Finance and the relevant State Secretary for Regional Economy. Notification has no longer been required in the

Walloon Region, however, since 1 January 2004 or in the Flemish Region since 1 January 2006.

Public Takeover Bids from Abroad

[27] Since 1 July 2003 and by contrast with the previous situation, any foreign company publicly offering its securities in Belgium without having a subsidiary or branch in Belgium is required to file its incorporation deed and its articles of association with the clerk of Brussels Commercial Court (section 88, Companies Code).

Foreign Exchange Legislation

[28] Currency exchange operations are regulated under sections 137 et seq. of the Act of 6 April 1995. From an institutional point of view, the exchange market is governed by the Act of 2 January 1991, on the Institut Belgo-Luxembourgeois du Change/Belgisch Luxemburgs Instituut voor de Wissel ('the Institute').

[29] Until 5 March 1990, there was a very flexible exchange control system for foreign currencies, based on a two-tier foreign exchange market controlled and administered by the Institute. The two markets were the regulated market, on which commercial transactions were effected, and the financial market, on which financial transactions were effected. In some cases, there was a choice as to the exchange market on which a transaction could be effected. However, this system was abolished in March 1990. Now, the Institute is entrusted with supervising foreign payments from and to the Belgian–Luxembourg Economic Union, and with implementing exchange controls. It also provides statistical information on the balance of payments of the Belgian–Luxembourg Economic Union.

General Provisions Relating to the Financial Services and Markets Authority ('FSMA')

[30] The CBFA, which was the product of integration of the Insurance Regulator with the Banking and Finance Commission, was the single regulatory body for the Belgian finance sector since 1 January 2004. It was replaced by the 'FSMA' on 1 April 2011, as a consequence of the adoption of the Twin Peaks legislation. The FSMA is an autonomous body endowed with legal personality and having its registered office in the administrative district of the Brussels-Capital Region.

[31] The functioning and composition of the FSMA are laid down in the Act of 2 August 2002 on regulation of the financial sector and financial services. These functions have undergone significant changes since the financial crisis. The Twin Peaks-reforms has consigned both the micro- and micro- prudential supervision of banks to the National Bank of Belgium. The FSMA, on the other hand, is responsible for the market conduct supervision.

[32] The FSMA is made up of four bodies: the chairman of the executive committee, the executive committee, the supervisory board and the penalties commission. The chairman of the executive committee steers the FSMA. He represents it in dealings with third parties and in legal proceedings. He is appointed by the King on the joint proposal of the Finance and Economy Ministers for a renewable term of six years. The supervisory board is made up of ten to fourteen members, appointed by the King on the joint proposal of the Minister of Finance and Economics for a renewable term of six years. The supervisory board members may not have been members of any other body of the FSMA during the five years preceding their appointment. The members decide which one of them will be the chairman of the supervisory board.

[33] Chaired by the chairman of the FSMA, the executive committee is responsible for:

- laying down the administration and management of the FSMA;
- appointing and recalling staff members;
- determining the policy orientation of the FSMA;
- laying down the general direction and priorities in relation to regulatory policy;
- laying down all measures pertaining to application of the statutory provisions within the FSMA's remit;
- in so far as required, rendering opinions on all legislative or regulatory bills affecting the FSMA's oversight remit; and

[34] Apart from the chairman, the executive committee is made up of three members.

[35] The penalties commission decides on the application of administrative sanctions.

[36] From 1 November 2015 and onwards the remit of the FSMA as set down in the Act of 2 August 2002 on regulation of the financial sector and financial services will cover the following:

- overseeing compliance with the rules to protect investor interests in relation to transactions involving financial instruments and ensuring the proper functioning, integrity and transparency of the securities markets;
- ensuring the oversight of investment advisers,, the management companies of collective investment bodies and exchange offices, companies involved in consumer financing, intermediaries in banking and investment services, regulated real estate companies, financial planners and credit suppliers;
- ensuring the oversight of insurance companies and insurance intermediaries;
- contributing to compliance with the rules aimed at protecting the general public and investors against the unlawful offering or provision of financial products or services;
- ensuring oversight of compliance with compliance with the various insurance regulation;
- ensuring oversight of compliance with the Act of 22 March 2006 on intermediation in banking and investment services;
- ensuring oversight of compliance with sections 77*bis* of the Act of 6 April 1995 on investment companies;
- ensuring oversight of undertakings subject to Royal Decree no. 43 of 15 December 1934 on the oversight of capitalization undertakings;

- ensuring oversight of compliance with title II, Chapter 1, sub-chapter 4 of the Finance Act of 24 December 2002, on occupational pensions for the self-employed; and
- ensuring oversight of compliance with the Supplementary Pensions Act and the tax rules governing such pensions and certain supplementary benefits in relation to social security.

[37] FSMA also has a number of extraterritorial powers.

[38] The Act of 16 June 2006 on public offerings of investment instruments and the admission of investment instruments to trading on regulated markets endows the FSMA with competence to approve prospectuses for certain offers of securities or admissions to trading outside Belgium. This extraterritorial competence on the FSMA's part results from the rules laid down by Directive 2003/71/EC. The new rules have the effect of repealing the old territoriality rules enshrined in the Act of 22 April 2003.

[39] In a similar vein, the new Takeover Bids Act of 1 April 2007 provides that the FSMA is competent for approving the prospectuses for certain offers involving securities of companies situated outside Belgium, in particular:

- voluntary public takeover bids involving listed voting securities of an offeree company whose registered office and principal market are both situated in another Member State;
- voluntary public takeover bids involving listed voting securities of an offeree company whose registered office is situated in Belgium, whose securities are admitted for trading on a Belgian regulated market and whose principal market is situated in another Member State; and
- voluntary public takeover bids involving listed voting securities of an offeree company whose registered office is situated in another Member State, whose securities are not admitted to trading on a regulated market and whose principal market is situated in Belgium.

[40] Finally, we would point out that, where a bid is launched simultaneously in two or more countries including Belgium, the prospectus approved in another Member State may in certain cases be recognized by the FSMA. Thus, the Takeover Bids Act of 1 April 2007 provides that the offeror may apply for the prospectus to be recognized where the bid is directed at voting securities admitted for trading on a regulated market provided the purpose of the bid is to acquire effective control of the offeree company. Along the same lines, the Act of 16 June 2006 on public issues of securities lays down the principle of the 'European passport', in terms of which any prospectus approved by the competent authority of the original Member State can be used in the other Member States. In this regard, it has to be pointed out that, in the case of a public takeover bid, the offeror must apply for recognition to the FSMA, which must give its consent and may require the offeror to add certain information aimed at protecting the general public in Belgium. However, in the case of a public issue of securities, it will be sufficient to notify an ad hoc dossier to the FSMA, which will have no prerogative to refuse recognition or demand the addition of certain information.

SPECIFIC RULES RELATING TO CORPORATE GOVERNANCE

Introduction

[41] The notion of corporate governance is an English notion that has been progressively integrated into the various continental European legal systems over the last fifteen years. Corporate governance covers organization of the control and management of an undertaking with the aim of establishing a better equilibrium between the shareholders and the management bodies of the company, who are required to ensure that no regard is taken of their personal interests.

[42] The notion was first used in Belgium in the 1990s. It is based on the idea that every company must be managed with the principal aim of increasing shareholder value. The notion may be extended much more widely nowadays to encompass all provisions relating to organization of the way in which a company functions and the division of powers amongst its various bodies. Ultimately, it was only on 9 December 2004 that the Belgian Code on Corporate Governance saw the light of day. The Code has then been subject to numerous amendments and adjustments taking account a number of positive and negative experiences with its previous versions, changes to the Belgian and European legal environment, as well as the changing expectations of the general public and of shareholders regarding the liability and conduct of companies and their directors. Consequently, a new version of the Code came out on 12 March 2009. The ultimate objective is to optimize the functioning of a company, first, by establishing a better balance for the board of directors and management and, second, by making the decisions of the board of directors more objective. It is thus a 'code of best practice'.

[43] This section deals with the key standards enacted in Belgium in this regard.

The Act of 13 April 1995 to Amend the Consolidated Commercial Companies Acts of 30 November 1935

[44] The Act of 13 April 1995 set up new rules to deal with conflicts of interests. The regulations in this area are of crucial importance in relation to corporate governance, since they are intended to avoid directors voting in relation to a transaction or decision affecting the company being influenced more by their personal interests than those of the company. Introduced by section 60 of the Consolidated Commercial Companies Acts, the rules are now to be found in section 523 of the Companies Code.

[45] Section 523 of the Companies Code lays down rules requiring a director with a direct or indirect interest of a financial nature in conflict with a decision or transaction falling within the remit of the board of directors to notify the other directors of the conflict of interests before the matter is debated by the board. Moreover, where such transactions or decisions concern a company that has made or makes public offers to investors, the director may not attend the deliberations of the board of directors relative thereto or take part in the ballot.

[46] The conditions for applying the conflicts of interests rules can be summarized as follows:

- the director must have an interest in conflict with the company's;
- conflicts of interests must be of a financial nature;
- the conflict of interests must be direct or indirect;
- the conflict of interests must exist in relation to a decision or transaction;
- the decision or transaction must fall within the remit of the board of directors.

[47] Faced with a conflict of interests situation, the director concerned is under a duty of information. The director is then prohibited from taking part in the debate and ballot relative to the transactions or decisions in question where they concern listed companies. Finally, the management report drawn up by the board of directors to the annual meeting of shareholders, must make mention of any conflict of interest that arose during the year, describe the nature of the decision or transaction in question and justify the decision taken and the financial consequences for the company.

The Act of 2 August 2002 Amending the Companies Code and the Act of 17 December 2008 Particularly Instituting Audit Committees in Listed Companies and Financial Undertakings

Introduction

[48] The Act of 2 August 2002 and the Act of 17 December 2008 introduced new provisions into the Companies Code making considerable changes in the field of corporate governance. These changes essentially concern the management and audit of companies and apply to both listed and unlisted companies. Some of these changes affect the prerogative the board of directors of a public limited liability company and authorizes the delegation of all or part of its management powers (with the exception of the general policy of the company and acts that are reserved to the board by statute) to an executive committee (sections 524*bis* Companies Code). The executive committee is furthermore accorded the status of an organ of the company. The Act of 2 August 2002 also sets down a new procedure entailing recourse to a committee of non-executive directors for transactions involving two or more companies in the same group.

The Executive Committee

[49] On condition it is expressly authorized to do so by the articles of association, the board of directors can delegate its management powers to an executive committee. Sections 524*bis*, first paragraph, uses the term 'authorizes' such that it seems to be ruled out that the articles can *require* the board of directors to delegate such powers to the executive committee. Once the powers have been delegated, however, the committee continues to be under the oversight of the board of directors. The committee, which is endowed with the status of an organ of the company, is made up of members of the board of directors or third parties, whereby the articles of association must indicate whether it is the shareholders in general meeting or the board of directors that have power to appoint them. The regime laid down by sections 524*bis* of the Companies Code is not therefore analogous to that set down by section 24 of the Act of 25 April 2014 on the status and control of credit institutions, since, under this statute, banks' executive committees may only be made up of directors. As already stated above, the powers delegated to the executive committee may not include the general policy of the company or the entire acts reserved by law to the board of directors. In this regard, definition has to be given to what parliament meant by the term 'general policy', on the one hand, and how far an act can be deemed to be 'reserved to the board of directors'.

[50] Since 'general policy' is not as such defined in the Companies Code, the notion requires to be defined more precisely in the articles of association. Otherwise, it seems to be possible to refer to the definition set down in the Protocol of 4 December 1997 on the autonomy of the banking function as regards credit institutions, in terms of which 'general policy includes the definition of main strategic thrusts of the credit institution, the adoption of plans and budgets, major structural reforms and definition of the relations between the credit institution and its shareholders'.

[51] As for the 'acts reserved' to the board of directors, this seems to refer to certain of the powers reserved specifically to the board of directors by the Companies Code. These powers particularly include the powers to call general meetings (section 532 Companies Code), propose amendments to the company's objects (section 559 Companies Code), propose amendments to the respective rights attaching to a class of shares (section 560 Companies Code), increase the share capital in terms of the authorized capital (sections 603 et seq. Companies Code) or propose the issue of shares at below accounting par (section 582 Companies Code). However, the fact that powers might be expressly conferred on the board of directors is not the sole criterion for concluding that they involve an 'act reserved' to the board of directors. Thus, where section 557, second paragraph, of the Companies Code states that the board of directors has the power to bring to a conclusion sufficiently committed transactions before receipt of the takeover bid opinion by the FSMA, the provision is not intended to attribute specific competence to the board of directors. Rather, it is intended to confirm the general competence of the board for all acts necessary or expedient for achieving the corporate objects of the company whereas, during a takeover bid period, that competence belongs solely to the general meeting. It can therefore be concluded that, in the case of a takeover bid, where such competence has been delegated to the executive committee, it will have power to pursue transactions sufficiently committed prior to the bid.

[52] The board of directors is charged with overseeing the executive committee. Hence, the board of directors may require the executive committee to pass it all information relating to decisions of a certain order of importance.

[53] Finally, the question arises whether the powers delegated by the board of directors to the executive committee are exclusive, or whether, by contrast, they are concurrent with the board's. There are several arguments from which it can be concluded that, by delegating such powers, the board disenfranchises itself since, first, section 26 of the Act of 22 March 1993, which inspired and is drafted in the same terms as sections 524*bis*, provided that the board cannot interfere in the powers of the committee. This still holds true in the Act of 25 April 2014. In addition, the fact that the law has provided that the executive committee should be liable for its own acts, thus discharging the board of directors from the consequences of the committee's decisions, only goes to support this idea. Finally, we would point out that the Dutch-language version of sections 524*bis* speaks of a transfer ('overdragen') of powers, and not delegation.

The Audit Committee

[54] As a general principle, the articles of association are free as to whether they provide for the creation of an audit committee, which is usually charged with a remit of overseeing the management of the company and its valuation and formulating proposals to improve its performance. Where an audit committee is set up, it does not constitute an organ of the company recognized by statute.

[55] The Act of 17 December 2008, published on 29 December 2008, introduced an obligation on certain listed public limited liability companies to set up an audit committee within their board of directors.

[56] This committee is composed of 'non-executive' directors, at least one member of which is 'independent' (cf. below) and that has particular powers in relation to the accounting and audit of the company (sections 526*bis* Companies Code).

[57] This obligation is limited to large-scale listed companies.

[58] For smaller-scale companies, the remit of the committee can be conferred on the board of directors if, and only if:

- the company has at least one independent director;
- and, where the chairman of the board is an 'executive' director, he does not chair the board when it is acting within the committee's remit (new sections 526*bis* (3) Companies Code).

[59] We would point out that a company will be deemed to be of smaller scale where it fulfils at least two of the following criteria:

- the average number of employees is less than 250 over the entire financial year in question;
- balance sheet total less than or equal to EUR43 000 000;
- net annual turnover less than or equal to EUR50 000 000.

[60] The audit committee's tasks cover at least the following:

- following up the effectiveness of the internal control systems;
- following up the effectiveness of the company's risk management;
- following up the effectiveness of the internal audit, where such a mechanism exists in the company concerned;
- following up statutory audit of the annual accounts and the consolidated accounts;

- following up the process of preparing financial information;
- examination and follow-up of the statutory auditor's independence – and that of the company auditor if there is one – charged with auditing the consolidated accounts, particularly in the context of additional services rendered to the company;
- nomination of the statutory auditor: if the board of directors continues to nominate the statutory auditor, this proposal must without fail be put forward on the basis of a 'pre-nomination' by the committee (section 533, last paragraph, Companies Code).

[61] Under sections 526*bis* (4), last paragraph, of the Companies Code, the committee regularly reports on its tasks to the board of directors.

Independent Directors

[62] The function of independent director is enshrined in section 524 of the Companies Code. Since the Act of 17 December 2008, the statutory requirements relating to the definition of 'independent' director have become even more stringent and demand fulfilment of the criteria set out in sections 526*ter* of the Companies Code:

1. during a period of five years preceding his appointment, he shall not have occupied an executive office in the board or any position as a member of the executive committee or as a person to whom the day-to-day management of the company was delegated, whether of the company or of any company or person linked thereto;

2. he shall not have sat on the board of directors as a non-executive director for more than three successive terms in office, whereby that period may not exceed twelve years (new criterion introduced by statute);

3. during a period of three years preceding his appointment, he shall not have formed part of the management personnel;

4. he shall not be in receipt of or have received remuneration or any other significant benefit of a financial nature from the company or from a company or partnership or person linked thereto within the meaning of section 11, other than directors' profit shares and fees that he may receive or have received as a non-executive member of the board or supervisory organ of the company;

5. he shall not hold any corporate rights representing one-tenth or more of the share capital, the assets of the company or any class of shares of the company;

6. he shall not maintain, or over the last accounting reference period have maintained, a significant business relationship with the company or a company or partnership or person linked thereto, whether directly or in the capacity of a member, shareholder, board member or management personnel member (new criterion introduced by statute);

7. he shall not during the last three years have been a partner or employee of the current or a previous external auditor of the company or of a company or partnership or person linked thereto (new criterion introduced by statute);

8. he shall not be an executive member of the board of another company in which an executive director of the company acts as an executive director of its board or member of its supervisory organ, or maintain other important links with the executive directors of the company by virtue of positions occupied in other companies or partnerships or organs;

9. he shall not have, either within the company or within a company or partnership or person linked thereto, either a spouse or legal cohabitant or parents or relatives up to the second degree occupying an office as member of the executive committee or as a person to whom the day-to-day management of the company is delegated or as a management personnel member or in any of the other cases set forth in points (1) to (8) by virtue of positions occupied in other companies or partnerships or organs (new criterion introduced by statute).

[63] The act by which independent directors are appointed must in each case provide evidence that these conditions are met. In this regard, the law presumes that each director who is a member of the executive committee or a person to whom day-to-day management of the company is delegated is an 'executive' (sections 526*bis* (3), third paragraph, Companies Code).

[64] We would point out that parliament has intentionally been very cautious as regards the criteria by which the independence of a director can be demonstrated.

[65] Although it is hardly likely that a company would subsequently cast question over a decision it had previously adopted, section 524(6) of the Companies Code provides that 'the company may act to set aside decisions taken or transactions carried out in breach of the rules set down in this section if the other party to such decisions or transactions had or ought to have had knowledge of such breach'. It is to be regretted that minority shareholders cannot implement such action.

[66] By contrast, if the procedures provided for in section 524 of the Companies Code have not been adhered to, then, under section 528 of the Companies Code, the directors are jointly liable either to the company or to third parties for all damages resulting from the breach committed.

[67] Moreover, even where the procedural rules have been followed, section 529 provides that 'the directors are personally and jointly liable for the loss sustained by the company or third parties further to decisions or transactions approved by the board, even where section 524 has been complied with, where such decisions or transactions have caused the company abusive financial prejudice to the benefit of a group company.'

[68] Accordingly, the directors can be held to be liable.

[69] As regards the minority shareholders, regard must be had to the provisions of section 562 of the Companies Code, which states that an action may be raised against directors on behalf of the company by the minority shareholders. This action is raised by one or more shareholders that, on the day on which quietus was pronounced in favour of the directors, possessed shares to which there attached 1% of the votes attaching to all the shares existing on that day or, on the same day, possessing shares representing a portion of the share capital equal to at least EUR1 250 000.

[70] Where an abusive financial benefit has been transferred to the detriment of the company, the directors will be personally and jointly liable and cannot seek refuge behind the fact that they might have voted against the measure. The only way to evade liability is if they resign their post before the decision is taken.

[71] Finally, we would point out that a further penalty may take the form of denunciation by the statutory auditor to the shareholders in general meeting and, as the case may be, a qualification expressed in the auditor's report or any other decision taken by him in light of the breach as found by him to exist. We come back in detail on the liability of directors below.

Independent Directors in Intra-Group Relations

[72] In terms of section 524 of the Companies Code as amended by the Act of 2 August 2002, certain transactions carried out in execution of a decision taken by a listed company must first be submitted for an assessment by a committee composed of three independent directors where it concerns other companies in the group. More particularly, decisions and transactions that are subject to such a procedure are those that concern:

- the company's relations with a related company, with the exception of transactions with its own subsidiaries (section 524(1), first paragraph (1°), Companies Code);
- the relations between a subsidiary of the said company and a company related thereto, other than a subsidiary of the said subsidiary (section 524(1), first paragraph (2), Companies Code).

[73] Section 524(5) goes on to state that decisions relative to the relations of an unlisted Belgian subsidiary of a listed Belgian company with a company related to the latter can only be taken with the authorization of the listed parent company. This authorization is also subject to the opinion of a committee of three independent directors.

[74] However, this procedure is not applicable to:

- decisions and transactions effected in the usual course of business under normal terms and normal market conditions for transactions of the same nature (section 524(1), third paragraph (1°), Companies Code);
- decisions and transactions representing less than 1% of the net asset value of the company as shown in the consolidated accounts (section 524(1), first paragraph (2°), Companies Code).

[75] We would point out that, on a combined reading of section 524 of the Companies Code and section 2(3°) of the Act of 2 August 2002, the procedure laid down in section 524 covers both companies listed abroad and Belgian companies.

[76] In the context of its remit, the committee of independent directors, assisted by one or more independent experts designated by it, describes the nature of the decision or transaction and assesses the gain or loss to the company and its shareholders, quantifies the financial consequences and finally examines whether or not the decision or transaction is such as to cause manifestly abusive loss to the company in the light of the policy conducted by the company. If the committee decides that the decision or transaction is not manifestly abusive but nevertheless causes prejudice to the company, the committee sets out the benefits that the decision or transaction will bring about to counter the prejudice referred to.

[77] The committee sends the board of directors a reasoned written opinion stating each element of assessment cited above. After taking cognisance of the opinion, the board of directors deliberates on the proposed decisions and transactions. If appropriate, where a director has a conflict of interests of a financial nature in relation to the decision or transaction, section 523 will apply. The board of directors states in its minutes whether the procedure described above has been adhered to and, as appropriate, the reasons on the basis of which the committee's opinion might have been deviated from. The statutory auditor gives an assessment of the reliability of the data figuring in the opinion and in the minutes of the board meeting. The statutory auditor's assessment is appended to the minutes of the board meeting. The decision of the committee, the extract from the minutes of the board meeting and the assessment by the statutory auditor are all incorporated into the management report to the shareholders.

[78] Since being amended by the Act of 2 August 2002, section 524 of the Companies Code no longer exclusively covers decisions falling within the competence of the board of directors. The question as to which of the company's organs must submit their decisions to this procedure remains a matter of controversy. In this respect, we believe that the decisions covered by the opinion do not encompass those within the competence of the shareholders in general meeting, since it seems improbable that parliament intended to require the general meeting to submit its decisions to the assessment of an independent committee of directors and a decision by the board of directors, whereas it is precisely the board of directors that is under a duty to render account to the general meeting and inform it of such management acts falling within the context of intra-group operations.

[79] The entire procedure laid down in section 524 of the Companies Code is the product of a broad process of reflection that has developed around the notion of corporate governance. Some commentators have encouraged consistent recourse to independent directors to ensure better autonomy of the board of directors as opposed to the reference shareholdership. The Act of 2 August 2002 nonetheless circumscribes the task of this type of directors just to decisions falling under section 524 of the Companies Code. However, in practice, independent directors will also be involved in other types of decisions in so far as they will usually be appointed beforehand and will sit on the board of directors as from their appointment. Moreover, the Belgian Code on Corporate Governance, which is analysed in the next section, recommends that listed companies should provide themselves with a board of directors made up of at least three independent directors.

Directors' Pay

[80] Directorships may be remunerated or unremunerated (section 517 Companies Code).

[81] Where the office is remunerated, the general meeting is the organ with exclusive authority to fix the amount of the emoluments of the board of directors. The articles of association have to specify whether the directors are entitled to such emoluments. Failing such, if they make no provision or fail to delegate this right to the general meeting, it is unable to grant them any remuneration.

[82] The directors' remuneration can take a variety of forms. The Belgian Code of Corporate Governance for its part says that the company must remunerate its executive directors and managers in an 'equitable and responsible' manner (Principle 7). It distinguishes between executive and non-executive directors. The latter receive only a fixed emolument linked to their directorship or certain specific roles such as that of chairman of the board of or of committees set up within the board, taking account of the responsibilities corresponding thereto and the time spent.

[83] Additional rules for listed companies have been introduced in the Companies Code by the Act of 6 April 2010. These rules bear a strong resemblance to the recommendations already contained in the 2009 Belgian Code of Corporate Governance (principle 7 and schedule F).

[84] Sections 526*quater* of the Companies Code provides that listed companies must set up a compensation committee within the board of directors. It is comprised of non-executive directors. There is an exception, however, for smaller companies, who have at least one independent director.

[85] The compensation committee has to draw up a report about the remuneration of the directors that has to be approved by the shareholders' meeting in accordance with section 554 of the Companies Code.

[86] According to sections 520*bis* of the Companies Code, all criteria on which variable payments of executive directors are based, must be listed in their contract or other documents that define the relation between them and the company. The payment of this variable salary is only allowed if these criteria are met. Non-executive directors can only be awarded variable payment with consent of the general shareholders' meeting (section 554 of the Companies Code).

[87] Moreover, sections 520*ter* of the Companies Code, prescribes that at least one-fourth of the variable remuneration must be based on objective criteria, which are established beforehand, and are measured during a period of at least two years. For another one-fourth, this period must be at least three years. Deviations from this rule is possible in the articles of association or with express permission of the general shareholders' meeting.

[88] Shares, which are given to directors of a listed company as part of their remuneration, can only be definitely acquired after a period of three years and options or other rights to acquire shares can only be exercised after three years, except if the articles of association deviate from this rule or with express permission of the general shareholders' meeting.

[89] Section 554 of the Companies Code provides that severance payments for executive directors, members of the executive committee, other leading persons according to the definition of section 96(3) or other persons in charge of the day-to-day management of listed companies should be limited to a maximum of twelve months' pay. Higher severance payments have to be approved by the general shareholders' meeting. Moreover, if the payment exceeds eighteen months' salary, a motivated opinion of the compensation committee is also required.

The Corporate Governance Codes

[90] By virtue of the very business they carry on, undertakings undergo constant change arising within the scientific and technical fields within which they operate. In meeting the risks thrown up by such change, companies must at any price equip themselves with an effective governance system and ensure that their officers administer the company optimally without regard to their purely personal interests.

[91] A large number of initiatives have been taken along these lines and, on 21 May 2003, the European Commission issued the Council and the Parliament with a communication setting out an action plan in relation to corporate governance. The communication states that it is up to each Member State to promulgate a standard code with which businesses must comply or requiring them explain how their practices differ and why.

[92] The growing importance placed on corporate governance principles resulted in Belgium in the 9 December 2004 publication of the Lippens Code. The Corporate Governance Commission charged with drawing up the Code recommended that the Belgian authorities should recognize it as the standard code for the purposes of the Commission communication.

[93] The most recent version of the Belgian Code of Corporate Governance dates from 12 March 2009. The Code is built on three types of rules: 'principles', 'provisions' and 'guidelines'. The 'principles', which are regarded as the pillars of good corporate governance and should be adhered to by companies in all cases without exception, are as follows:

- the company should adopt a clear corporate governance structure;
- the company should set up un effective, efficient board of directors that takes decisions in the interests of the company;
- all the directors should act with integrity and commitment;
- the company should set up a rigorous, transparent procedure for the appointment and assessment of the board of directors and its members;
- the board of directors should set up specialist committees;
- the company should define a clear executive management structure;
- the company should remunerate its directors and executive managers in an equitable and responsible manner;
- the company should respect the rights of all the shareholders and encourage their participation; and
- the company should ensure that its corporate governance policy is suitably publicized.

[94] Breach of any of these principles carries no sanction other than that of the market. However, having said so, this does nothing to make them any less obligatory to the extent that such sanctions are just as serious as a legal penalty imposed on a listed company.

[95] Furthermore, each of these 'principles' is linked to 'provisions', which describe how they are to be applied. Companies must comply or at least give justification for the reasons and special circumstances why they do not ('comply or explain'). Each of these 'provisions' is in turn accompanied by guidelines, which describe how companies are to apply the provisions. Intended as simple advice, they are not subject to the 'comply or explain' obligation.

[96] On 18 November 2005, a bill was tabled before parliament aimed at extending the joint and several liability of company directors as laid down in section 528 of the Companies Code. This tightening of the liability rules would enable any third party alleging loss to raise court proceedings against directors failing to adhere to the corporate governance rules enacted by the company.

[97] Moreover, because corporate governance does not just concern listed companies, a code intended for unlisted companies was officially issued on 21 September 2005: before such a code might be enacted, good governance recommendations had met with little response from SMEs to the extent that they were of less practical application to this sort of business. However, because the management system of an SME has significant impact on its growth, the SME organizations in Belgium, the Union des Classes Moyennes (UCM) and the Unie van Zelfstandige Ondernemers (UNIZO) took the initiative of setting up a 'corporate governance commission for unlisted companies'. The Commission, placed under the chairmanship of Baron Paul Buysse, was given the task of drawing up a code intended for unlisted companies.

[98] The Commission tabled its draft code on 21 March 2005. There was considerable reaction to it, stemming *inter alia* from all the major parties involved in corporate governance. The reactions were incorporated into the wording of the final Code, which was officially issued on 21 September 2005.

[99] Though related to the Lippens Code, the Buysse Code is more voluntary in nature and is not based on the 'comply or explain' principle

SPECIFIC RULES RELATING TO SMEs LISTED AT A STOCK EXCHANGE

Introduction

[100] Given the fundamental notion that a company has to be worth at least EUR50 mn for its listing on a classic regulated market to be of interest, a large number of small and medium-sized enterprises are de facto excluded from those markets. These companies may nevertheless want to benefit from the access to funding that follows from participation in a financial market. It was with this in mind that the Free Market and Alternext were launched in Brussels.

[101] These two markets bring together smaller-scale enterprises and offer them easier conditions of access to the market, whilst ensuring that investors' needs in terms of transparency and liquidity are properly catered for. Such markets also offer good investment opportunities from the point of view that the companies they are aimed at are often involved in the development of attractive and innovative products.

The Free Market

[102] The Free Market is an unregulated market that was launched by Euronext Brussels in 2004. Self-regulation was thus considered as the requisite solution to the problem of how to get round the impossibility for the majority of SMEs to access the benefits of stock-market listing. Applying principles of self-regulation is based on the idea that any system of regulation is susceptible to distortion and, hence, all systems are dependent on the trust of the various market players. On the basis of this given, it was therefore proposed launching a flexible market based exclusively on investor trust in issuers, the essential features of which are explained below.

No Particular Conditions for Admission

[103] Companies that want to join the Free Market can be admitted without having to satisfy certain market capitalization or floating capital thresholds. Companies also do not have to meet certain criteria in terms of turnover and return on investment. Nor does Euronext Brussels impose any conditions as to profile or business sector. Accordingly, the Free Market is open to enterprises active in any economic sector, regardless of size or performance. It nonetheless remains the case that, in order to secure funding from the general public, a company has to prove to them that it possesses particular know-how in its domain and thus offer attractive growth prospects.

Issuer's Obligation

[104] The fact that this market is not regulated has a number of implications. First, it means that there exists no duty of information. No information obligation is imposed on companies listed on this market, and hence issuers are not subject to a duty to disclose periodic and occasional information. However, because a system of self-regulation can only function on the basis of investor trust, issuers must ensure that this is upheld by regularly disclosing certain information to bring to investors' knowledge data relative to the financial health of the companies they finance. The FSMA furthermore recommends that companies listed on such a market should appoint a statutory auditor to audit and certify their accounts. Ultimately, although the FSMA cannot intervene to prevent and discipline insider trading and price manipulation by companies listed on the market, the criminal penalties for such acts are nonetheless still applicable.

[105] Issuers do continue to be subject to an obligation to publish a prospectus where they call for funds from the public in excess of EUR2.5 m. Commission Regulation

809/2004 of 29 April 2004, implementing Directive 2003/71/EC, sets out the various types of information that must be included in the prospectus, the structure it has to adhere to, the procedures for its publication, and the procedure for issuing promotional messages and including information by reference. Approval of the prospectus at the time the company is introduced onto the Free Market is therefore the sole, albeit far from negligible, involvement of the FSMA in verifying information issued by a company listed on that market. Once it is admitted to trading, its sole obligation is to lodge its annual accounts with the National Bank of Belgium.

Trading Rules

[106] The Free Market is accessible to all members of Euronext Brussels. Deals are carried out per unit in one single fixing per session, at 3 p.m. (principal lines), 3.30 p.m. (secondary lines) or 4 p.m. (obligations). Deals effected in the central order book are automatically reported to Euronext Brussels via the trading system (NSC).

[107] Purchase and sale orders are disseminated and matched and the market data relative thereto transmitted using the trading and information transmission systems of Euronext.

Deal Settlement and Delivery

[108] Once the offer is made, the buyer gives an irrevocable undertaking to take delivery of the securities and settle the price whilst the seller irrevocably undertakes to deliver the securities and receive payment.

Alternext

[109] Alternext is a market that was launched in Belgium by Euronext Brussels in June 2006. Aimed at small and medium-sized enterprises, and thus forming a complement to the Free Market, creation of this market is a supplementary means by which this type of undertaking can access the market.

Admission Conditions

[110] In principle, any small or medium-sized enterprise may apply for listing on the Alternext market on condition it effectively opens up its capital in the form of a private placement or public offering.

[111] If the opening of capital takes the form of a private investment, it must have taken place within two years preceding the application for admission and must amount to at least EUR2.5 mn. Furthermore, at least three shareholders must hold shares in the company before it is admitted to listing. If the opening takes the form of a public offering, it must result in subscription of a minimum sum of EUR2.5 mn and requires to be effected through the offices of a duly accredited investment services provider. The public issue of shares will additionally give rise to publication of a prospectus, whereas only an information memorandum is required in the case of a private placement of shares.

[112] In the case of an issue of shares of the same class of securities as are already admitted to listing, an admission application has to be made for them. The application has to be made at the time the securities are issued if they are issued as part of a public offering, and within ninety days in other cases.

Issuer's Obligations

[113] Once its securities are admitted to listing, the issuer must ensure equality of treatment as between all holders of securities that are held under the same conditions and provide them with all information necessary for exercise of their rights. Apart from the publicity measures required in Belgium in the context of a public call for savings, a certain amount of information must be publicly disclosed by the issuer, such as its annual report, the management report prepared within four months of its balance sheet date, amendments of rights attaching to its securities, upward or downward crossing of the holding thresholds of 25%, 50%, 75% or 95% and, finally, precise information concerning one or more issuers of financial instruments that, if rendered public, will be likely to significantly affect the price of the financial instruments in question or those connected thereto. We would furthermore point out that the issuer must make provision for all this information to be made available on a distinct part of its or Alternext's site, and make sure it is kept on line for three years.

[114] In addition, the issuer must inform Euronext Brussels three months beforehand of alterations in the number of securities issued and changes to the trading system.

Trading Rules

[115] The trading and conduct rules applicable on Alternext are those that govern the regulated Euronext markets and are contained in Chapters 4 and 8 of book I of the Euronext rules. Thus, at the free choice of the investor and the intermediary and by joint agreement between them, the interests of buyers and sellers are matched according to one of the following mechanisms:

- multilateral matching in a central order book;
- bilateral matching with the interests of an identified counterparty;
- bilateral matching with the interests of a market maker.

[116] Deals effected by bilateral matching are deemed effected on Alternext where the buy instruction and the corresponding sell instruction are matched under the conditions set out below.

[117] If deals take place via the central order book, they have to be effected in accordance with Chapter 4 of book I of the Euronext rules and the Manual of Dealings on Securities Markets, especially in relation to the securities for which orders are accepted by the system and the principles of transparency. Thus, the Manual lays down the conditions for the classification of traded securities by single fixing and those that are fixed continuously. The most liquid shares are traded continuously between 9 a.m. and 5.30 p.m. whereas, for the less liquid ones, a price maximizing the number of securities traded is fixed once a day at 3.30 p.m. The trading times and associated reservation thresholds are furthermore set down in the schedule to the Manual.

[118] However, if the parties wish to match their interests outside the central order book and they are granted an identified counterparty, they can make use of the TCS system. Those wishing to deal using this system have to indicate the declarant's and counterparty's identifiers, the quote identifier, the price, the quantity and the type of instruction. This system is open between 7.15 a.m. and 7 p.m. and, for every deal carried out, Euronext reports the quote identifier, price, quantity, date and time.

[119] The members of the system are also able to opt to trade with market makers, which, for a minimum amount of EUR5 000, continuously offer indicative spreads of purchase and sale prices in relation to securities on which they declare themselves to be market makers, thus favouring the liquidity of the securities. In return, they benefit from publicity for their references on the Euronext web site and access to the Alternext price display system. However, they do not in any event benefit from any exclusivity as to the securities in question.

Deal Settlement and Delivery

[120] Once the offer is made, the buyer gives an irrevocable undertaking to take delivery of the securities and settle the price whilst the seller irrevocably undertakes to deliver the securities and receive payment.

SPECIFIC RULES RELATING TO LIABILITY UNDER COMPANY LAW

Founders' Liability

Introduction

[121] Once the shareholders have decided to incorporate a company, and to the extent it is not incorporated by way of public subscription, they are under an obligation to be present or represented before a notary public for execution of the solemn deed of incorporation of the company. The parties to the deed are generally deemed to be the founders of the company. However, section 450 of the Companies Code states that, if the deed of incorporation designates one or more shareholders that together hold a third or more of the share capital of the company as founders, the other parties, whose involvement is limited to signing the deed without directly or indirectly receiving any particular benefit, are deemed to be simple subscribers. It is thus important to distinguish between the 'subscriber parties' and the 'founder subscribers', as only the latter incur liability.

Liability

[122] The founders are liable for the valid incorporation of the company and must compensate losses resulting from any irregularity.

[123] This liability translates first of all into a guarantee obligation incumbent on all the founders. As a guarantor of due performance of the obligations of the other founders, each founder is jointly and severally liable for payment of the following amounts:

- any portion of share capital that is not validly subscribed owing to the invalidity of a subscription or by reason of the fact that it is not able to be represented by the share capital or is of no value;
- any negative difference between the statutory minimum and the amount of all the subscriptions together;
- compulsory amounts requiring to be paid up;
- in the case of a private limited liability company (*société privée à responsabilité limitée/besloten vennootschap met beperke aansprakelijkheid*), the sum required to pay up one-fifth of the value of the shares issued upon the incorporation of the company in exchange of cash contributions and the sum required to fully pay up shares issued in exchange of contributions in kind, (section 223 of the Companies Code);
- the sum required to pay up shares subscribed directly or by means of certificates in breach of section 217 of the Companies Code;
- in the case of a public limited liability company (*société anonyme/naamloze vennootschap*), the sum required to pay up one-fourth of the value of the shares issued upon the incorporation of the company in exchange of cash contributions or contributions in kind, it being understood that shares issued in exchange of contributions in kind must be fully paid up within five years from the date of the incorporation of the company (section 448 of the Companies Code);
- the sum required to pay up the portion of share capital which they are deemed to be subscribers.

[124] Furthermore, the founders will be liable and have to make good any loss resulting from:

- the nullity of the company, as pronounced by application of section 227 or section 454 of the Companies Code;
- the absence or inaccuracy of the information required by section 226 or sections 451 and 453 of the Companies Code;
- manifest overvaluation of contributions in kind;
- the damages provided for by section 65 of the Companies Code;
- the manifest insufficiency, at the time of the incorporation, of the share capital to support the business of the company for at least two years, should the company be declared bankrupt within three years from its incorporation.

[125] In this last case, the court will fix the commitments of the company for which the founders are liable. Moreover, in assessing the manifestly insufficient nature of the share capital, the court must take a view as at the time of incorporation of the company and take into account the assessment factors that the founders had knowledge of at that time, when fixing the amount of the share capital. Thus, the founders cannot be held liable where it is apparent that the company's insolvency is the result of later management errors.

Liability of the Directors of a Belgian Limited Liability Company

General Rules of Liability

[126] According to section 522 of the Companies Code, the board of directors is empowered to take any action necessary or useful for accomplishment of the company's objects, except for powers reserved to the general shareholders' meeting by law or by the articles of association.

[127] If a directorship is held by a legal entity, pursuant to section 61(2) of the Companies Code, it has to designate an individual from among its shareholders, directors, business managers, management committee members or employees as a permanent representative charged with carrying out the directorship duties in the name and for the account of the legal entity. In that case, the permanent representative bears the same (civil and criminal) liability as the legal entity appointed as director.

[128] As a rule, a director is not personally responsible for contractual arrangements entered into by him on behalf of the company (section 61(1), Companies Code). This is an important limitation on the potential liability of directors. Hence, acts committed by them in their capacity as company directors will be imputed to the company and in principle the director himself cannot be held contractually liable for such acts.

[129] The legal framework in which the directors may be held to be liable in tort towards third parties is less certain, however. The cases decided by the Court of Cassation in this respect illustrate very well the underlying difficulties in this field. In a case decided on 29 June 1989, the Court initially took the view that third parties suffering loss due to breach of a duty of care committed by a board could validly sue that organ, albeit on the proviso that the breach did not constitute a simple management error. In a later case decided on 7 November 1997, the Court went on to stipulate that 'where a contracting party acts through an organ, employee or agent for the performance of its contractual obligation, the latter may only be held liable in tort if the breach of a duty of care on which its liability is founded constitutes failure to obtemper a general obligation of prudence and that failure has caused a loss other than that resulting from poor performance of the contract'. However, in its 16 February 2001 decision, the Court took the stance that 'where an organ of a company or an office-holder acting within the framework of his mandate commits a breach of a duty of care that does not constitute an intentional tort in the course of negotiations giving rise to signature of a contract, that breach does not render the director or office-holder liable, but rather the company or principal'. With this decision, the Court thus appeared to break with the traditional solution that the liability of the organ is not overridden by that of the company. Nonetheless, in a judgment of 20 June 2005, the Court stated that 'if the breach of a duty of care committed by the organ of a company during the course of negotiations prior to signature of a contract incurs the direct liability of that legal person, that liability does not automatically rule out the personal liability of the organ, but *co-exists* along therewith'. Now, therefore, it is necessary to determine under what conditions such liability can again coexist with that of the legal person. In this regard, there is nothing in the 20 June 2005 decision from which it can be concluded that the Court intended to cast any question over the principles enshrined in its first two judgments, and so the interpretation in relation thereto can be transposed to the Court's new dicta. Thus, a director cannot be held liable in tort towards third parties unless the breach of duty of care and the loss sued for are purely 'tortious', and therefore do not flow either from the contract between the third party and the legal person or from the mandate existing between the legal person and the organ.

[130] Outside the bounds of this general liability framework, the directors can in any event be liable for errors in certain specific cases set forth in the Companies Code, as explained below.

Liability for Mismanagement ('actio mandati')

[131] According to section 527 of the Companies Code, the directors, members of the management committee and persons in charge of the day-to-day management of the company are liable under general civil law principles for performance of their duties and acts of mismanagement. The relationship between the company and a director is considered to be of a contractual nature, whereby the director becomes the company's agent/representative pursuant to the shareholders' decision to appoint him. The standard of care required of a director of a company is therefore customarily judged under the general principles of agency law. A director is thus held to the standard of care required of a normally careful person acting in such a position and in the same situation. The duties of a director are 'best efforts' obligations ('obligation de moyens' or 'middelenverbintenis').

[132] Since a director is accountable to the company for his management, only the company, i.e., the shareholders' meeting, deciding by simple majority, may invoke the directors' liability for acts of mismanagement pursuant to the actio mandati (section 561, Companies Code). However, in certain circumstances, the company's creditors may institute an actio mandati in lieu of the company if they can demonstrate that the company has acted to the detriment of their rights by not instituting an actio mandati or by giving a release, effectively blocking any *actio mandati*, e.g., in cases where it was clear that the company was entitled to recover damages. This action is based upon section 1166 of the Civil Code, which provides that creditors may exercise the rights and claims of their debtors, except for those that are exclusively related to the debtor's person. If the company is declared bankrupt, this action will be available to the trustee-in-bankruptcy or the creditors.

[133] The decision by a company to sue any of its directors for acts of mismanagement must be taken by a majority of shareholders. However, pursuant to sections 562-565 of the Companies Code, a minority shareholder or a group of small shareholders has the right to sue the directors on behalf of the company. For this purpose, the minority must consist of one or more shareholders who, on the date of the annual shareholders' meeting which considered releasing the director or directors concerned, together owed securities: (i) representing on that date at least 1% of the voting rights then in existence; or (ii) representing at that time a fraction of the share capital amounting to at least EUR1 250 000. The only shareholders that may be party to the action are those that, at the relevant annual meeting of shareholders, did not vote in favour of releasing the directors from their liability or voted in favour of a release that was subsequently held invalid in court.

[134] It has been held that the following constitute simple management errors for which a director will only be held liable toward the company:

- failure to attend meetings of the board of directors;
- failure to take measures necessary to mitigate the consequences of contractual non-performance;
- incurring exaggerated advertising expenditure;
- payment of a debt not due;
- granting loans or payment terms without adequate guarantees;
- failure to pursue debtors of the company with the necessary diligence;
- failure to exercise sufficient oversight over a person to whom day-to-day management of the company is delegated or to delegate the day-to-day management of the company to a competent person;
- entering into a contract under terms that are manifestly unfavourable to the company;
- contracting with a non-registered building contractor;
- failure to carry out formalities necessary to obtain payment of a subsidy for which the company qualifies;
- various failures in the management of the company's affairs, such as failing to protest an erroneous invoice in due time, making unadvised investments, firing a staff member without cause and thus obliging the company to bear the burden of a serious severance settlement, etc.
- issuing invoices containing inaccurate particulars.

Liability for Violation of Company Law or the Articles of Association

[135] According to section 528 of the Companies Code, directors are jointly and severally liable both to the company and to third parties for any loss suffered by them resulting from breach of the provisions of: (i) the Companies Code; and (ii) the articles of association of the company.

[136] In such cases, any director or member of the management committee in office at the time of the breach is deemed jointly and severally liable with the other directors or member of the management committee for damages unless he proves that he did not participate in the breach or that he was not negligent, for instance because he was justifiably absent and did not know about the situation and, if he became aware of the breach, disclosed it at the next meeting of shareholders called thereafter (section 528(3) of the Companies Code). The joint and several liability of the directors is therefore not absolute.

[137] In the event a breach of the Companies Code or the articles of association of the company constitutes breach of an absolute obligation (obligation de résultat/ resultaatsverbintenis), assessment of the breach will not be problematic. On the other hand, some provisions of the Companies Code or the articles of association instead qualify as best efforts obligations (obligation de moyens/middelenverbintenis) on the part of the directors. In such cases, the Belgian courts apply the standard test of the normally prudent and diligent director.

[138] Thus, the following have been held to constitute breaches of the Companies Code:

- any breach of accounting law committed in preparing the annual accounts (insufficient depreciation, lack of provisions, overvaluation of assets, failure to mention sureties granted in favour of third parties, etc.);
- failure to call a general meeting in the event of loss of over half the share capital (violation of section 633, Companies Code);
- carrying out a capital reduction by repayment to the shareholders without complying with the deadlines laid down by sections 612 et seq. of the Companies Code;
- failure to publish notice of the appointment or recall/resignation of directors;
- failure to comply with section 629 of the Companies Code on the prohibition against loans and securities granted by a company for the purpose of acquisition of its shares or profit-sharing certificates;
- irregularities in the functioning of the organs of the company such as the failure to hold a meeting of the board of directors or a general meeting of shareholders, failure to prepare minutes;
- refusal to provide the statutory auditors with information they are entitled to demand under section 137 of the Companies Code;
- noncompliance with the legal provisions applying in the case of conflicts of interests;
- noncompliant administration of the register of shareholders;
- fictitious subscription of the share capital – immediate repayment of paid-up capital to the remitting subscribers.

Directors' Liability in the Event of Bankruptcy

[139] According to section 530(1) of the Companies Code, in the event of bankruptcy and lack of assets, any director or former director and any other person who effectively had power to manage the company may be declared personally liable, jointly or severally, for all or part of the company's liabilities to the extent that they exceed its assets if it is established that clear, gross negligence on the part of such person contributed to the bankruptcy.

[140] The right to sue the directors or de facto directors for damages resulting from insufficient assets in cases of bankruptcy can be exercised by the trustee-in-bankruptcy or by a creditor. He must prove that there has been clear, gross negligence on the part of the defendant. It is not required to establish a causal relationship between the gross negligence and the bankruptcy. However, the court has power to limit the defendant's personal liability if, in the circumstances, it appears unreasonable to hold him liable for all debts exceeding the company's assets.

[141] In addition, the directors can be held liable for any increase in the company's debts resulting from a belated declaration of the company's bankruptcy.

[142] Finally, the Act of 20 July 2006, as published in the Belgian official gazette of 28 July 2006, introduced a new section 530(2) to the Companies Code, pursuant to which directors or former directors and any other persons who effectively had power to manage the company can be held personally and jointly liable for all or part of the social security contributions due by the company when it has been declared bankrupt, if it is established that clear, gross negligence on the part of such persons caused the bankruptcy or that such persons have been involved, within a period of five years preceding the company's bankruptcy, in at least two bankruptcies, liquidations or similar operations resulting in social security contributions being due.

Liability of Directors in the Case of Insufficient Identification of the Company

[143] Pursuant to section 80 of the Companies Code, a director (and, in fact, any person acting for and on behalf of the company) may, depending on the circumstances, be held personally liable for all contractual arrangements entered into by him on behalf of the company by virtue of a deed, invoice or other corporate document that fails to mention certain mandatory information concerning the company such as its name and form, the address of its registered office and its registration number with the Crossroads Bank of Enterprises, to the extent that the party to the arrangement has been misled as to the identity of the contracting party.

[144] In addition, section 79 of the Companies Code provides that, if the instrument states the amount of the company's share capital, reference must be made to the paid-up capital according to the latest balance sheet. If the paid-up capital is no longer intact, reference must be made to the net assets reflected in the latest balance sheet. Section 79 of the Companies Code further provides that, if a higher amount is mentioned and the company fails to perform according to contract, the third party may claim damages from the person who executed the relevant instrument so as to restore him to the position he would have been in had the relevant amount of share capital been mentioned.

Liability for Non-payment of Wage Withholding Tax ('Income Tax Deducted at Source') and/or VAT

[145] The Act of 20 July 2006, as published in the Belgian official gazette of 28 July 2006, introduced special rules pursuant to which directors or former directors and any other persons who effectively had power to manage the company can, under particular circumstances, be held jointly liable for repeated for non-payment of wage withholding tax ('income tax deductions at source') and VAT and, as mentioned above, in the case of the company's bankruptcy, outstanding social security contributions.

Liability of Directors in Cases of Personal Interests

[146] According to section 529 of the Companies Code, the company and any third party who has suffered loss may hold the directors liable if any director has gained an unjustified benefit to the detriment of a company from an operation or resolution approved by the board of directors in respect of which he had a direct or indirect personal interest. In such a case, the directors are jointly and severally liable even though the provisions of the relevant section 523 of the Companies Code, applicable in the event of personal interests of directors, have been complied with.

[147] If this procedure has not been complied with, all the directors will be jointly and severally liable for the company's breach in accordance with the principles set out in section III above.

Liability of the Directors for Overvaluation in the Case of an Acquisition of Assets from Shareholders or Directors

[148] According to section 458 of the Companies Code, the directors may be held jointly and severally liable for losses which are the direct and immediate consequence of the acquisition of assets by the company from its shareholders or directors within two years after incorporation for a price which is at least equal to one-tenth of the stated share capital, if such consideration is found to be clearly excessive.

Liability of the Directors in the Case of a Capital Increase

[149] Section 610 of the Companies Code stipulates that the directors in office at the time of an increase in the company's share capital will be jointly and severally liable for:

- the amount of the capital increase which has not been validly subscribed for– in such a case, the directors are deemed to subscribe themselves;
- any amount by which the contribution in kind or cash falls short of one-fourth of the shares; actual payment within a term of five years for any shares that wholly or partially relate to contributions in kind, as well as payment of the part of the share capital to which the directors are deemed to subscribe according to the preceding paragraph;
- payment for shares subscribed to, directly or through certificates, in breach of the prohibition against a company subscribing for its own shares (as referred to in section 585 of the Companies Code); and
- direct and immediate damages resulting either from the absence or incorrectness of mandatory information in the case of a capital increase pursuant to a public offer (as referred to in section 590 of the Companies Code), or from the manifest overvaluation of contributions in kind.

Liability in a Case of Conversion of Company Form

[150] Pursuant to section 785 of the Companies Code, the directors of a company whose legal form is converted are, notwithstanding any contrary provision, jointly and severally liable to the parties concerned:

- to pay any difference between the net assets of the company after conversion and the mandatory minimum share capital amount;
- for any overvaluation of the net assets shown in the prior statement of assets and liabilities referred to in section 776 of the Companies Code;
- to compensate them for any immediate and direct losses resulting either from nullity pursuant to non-observance of certain specific rules, or from the absence or incorrectness of specific statements to be made at the time of the conversion.

Criminal Liability

[151] Various breaches of company law by directors carry criminal penalties, including but not limited to the following:

- failure by the directors to submit the annual accounts to the shareholders within six months of the end of the financial year (section 92, Companies Code);
- failure by the directors to prepare the management report to be submitted to the shareholders at the annual shareholders' meeting, or to include certain mandatory information in that report, or failure to prepare the necessary reports relative to a merger, division or contribution of a line of business (section 647, Companies Code);
- breach by the directors of the rules concerning the distribution of interim dividends (section 648, Companies Code).

[152] The Companies Code also imposes criminal penalties in the form of fines or imprisonment or both, on certain breaches of the Companies Code committed with fraudulent intent.

[153] It should be noted that, according to section 5 of the Criminal Code, a legal entity is criminally liable for any offences inextricably related to the accomplishment of its objects or the preservation of its interests or which, in the circumstances, have been committed on its behalf. If an individual wilfully and knowingly commits an offence, he may be held jointly liable along with the company. Of course, a director (or employee) who acts solely in his own interests and not in the interests of the company will still be held personally liable for criminal offences even if they are committed in performance of his directorship duties (or employment contract).

[154] The directors may also be held criminally liable under, amongst others, sections 492*bis* of the Criminal Code for misappropriation of company funds and goods (abus de biens sociaux/misbruik van vennootschapsgoederen).

[155] Practical examples of the misappropriation of company funds include use of company funds or the company's credit for private purposes, the allocation of unjustified remuneration or benefits in kind, etc.

Liability of the Liquidators

[156] As the organ charged with liquidation of a company, the liquidators carry out a certain number of acts of management and disposal for which they bear personal liability. Whereas third parties may play no part in their designation, the liquidators are liable to them for proper performance of their duties. Moreover, the liquidators are naturally contractually liable for breaches of duties of care vis-à-vis the company.

[157] Parallel to this civil liability, liquidators are liable to criminal prosecution and fines where they fail to send the commercial court for the judicial district where the company's registered office is situated a detailed memorandum on the state of the liquidation. Sections 189*bis*, introduced by the Act of 2 June 2006 amending the Companies Code to improve liquidation procedures, requires liquidators to send a detailed memorandum on the state of the liquidation, composed at the end of the sixth and twelfth month of the first year of the liquidation, to the commercial court's registry during the seventh and thirteenth months after the start of the liquidation and once a year from the second year. Following a hearing, the court can furthermore replace a liquidator that fails to submit such a detailed statement. Sections 189*bis* is not applicable if the dissolution and liquidation take place in one deed in accordance with section 184(5) of the Companies Code.

MOST COMMON TYPES OF TRANSACTIONS

[158] The form of transaction employed will necessarily depend on the type of investment or cooperation contemplated. The transaction will take the form of a transfer of either assets or shares, possibly resulting in a merger. If the intention of the parties is to coordinate the activities of two undertakings, the transaction will generally take the form of a merger, whereas, if a less intensive level of cooperation is intended, the transaction may simply involve the acquisition of joint or mutual interests or interlocking shareholdings. These various possibilities are considered below.

Private Acquisition Agreements

[159] In many cases, the purchaser will be dealing with a single shareholder or a group of shareholders from which the assets or all the shares of the relevant company will be purchased. These transactions, which are very common, will lead to negotiation of specific warranties, which are not provided for under the general principles of law applicable to sale agreements. It is customary to limit the amount or value of such warranties and to limit their duration (two years for general warranties and a duration equal to the statute of limitation for warranties relating to tax). Even third parties can demand warranties in cases of mergers or demergers by private acquisition falling under the specific provisions of the Companies Code. For instance, third-party contractors of merged or divided companies may require specific warranties, the terms of which may be determined by the president of the commercial court if the parties themselves cannot reach agreement.

Takeover Bids

[160] Public takeover bids are governed by the Takeover Bids Act of 1 April 2007 and its two implementing Royal Decrees of 27 April 2007. As already indicated above, the aim of this Act was to transpose Directive 2004/25/EC of 21 April 2004 on takeover bids into Belgian law.

[161] According to the Takeover Bids Act of April 2007 and the Royal Decrees of 27 April 2007 compulsory bids are based on the criterion of breach of a threshold, and no longer, as before, on the acquisition of control of the offeree company. Thus, any person that, by virtue of an acquisition of shares in a company, acquires 30% of the voting securities of that company is bound to launch a bid for the entire voting shares and securities conferring voting rights in relation to the company.

Other Forms of Changes in Majority

[162] Depending on the precise circumstances of each particular case, other forms of transfer or methods of securing control may be possible. These may, where appropriate, be combined with the alternatives mentioned above. For example, control may change hands following an increase in the share capital of the company. This would be the case where the offeree company carried out a financial restructuring to reduce its capital by an amount equal to its accumulated losses, immediately followed by an increase in its capital, to be issued only to new shareholders.

Transfer of Shares or Assets

[163] A transfer of assets or parts of a business offers the following advantages compared to a transfer of shares:

(a) the purchaser will be entitled in the first year to depreciate the assets transferred in line with their acquisition value, whereas shares purchased may, under certain conditions, only be subject to impairment;
(b) the transferee will not be liable for the past debts of the company (with the exception of certain employees' rights in the case of a transfer of undertaking);
(c) the transferee will be in a better position to create charges over the assets transferred; Belgian company law in fact prohibits the rendering of financial assistance under the conditions set out below;
(d) the transferee is not restricted by the presence of minority shareholders, whose interests would have had to be taken into account if the transferee were to acquire control of the company by purchasing its shares.

[164] However, a transfer of assets entails the following drawbacks:

(a) the transferor will normally be liable to tax on the capital gain arising from the transfer, whether the gain results from a liquidation or a regular sale. However, the same taxation principles will also apply upon a transfer of shares if the shareholding is linked to the business of the transferor. Where the shares are held by an individual, the capital gain will be exempt from taxation unless the transfer is made to a foreign company;

(b) a transfer of real property will be subject to the payment of registration duties at a rate of 12.5% in Brussels and Wallonia and 10% in Flanders of the value of the property transferred.

(c) parties who have contracted with the transferor will not be obliged to continue the contractual relationship with the new entity, since Belgian law does not provide for the automatic transfer of contracts. While this question is generally a theoretical issue, it has led to a number of legal actions (in which the court has reaffirmed the principle that contractual obligations cannot automatically be assigned). However, since the Act of 13 April 1995, the contribution and the transfer of a line of business or of all the assets of an undertaking has been regulated by law. This act constitutes Titles III and IV of Book XI of the Companies Code.

[165] The similarity between a transfer of assets and mergers and divisions has thus been enshrined by parliament, which has consolidated the laws relating to these matters into one single body of law. Transfers of businesses (fonds de commerce/handelszaak) are not covered by this legislation as such, so that the old principles and rules continue to apply to such transfers;

[166] The choice between these two forms of transfer will therefore depend on the nature of the undertaking and its assets, as well as on the fiscal consequences and the objectives of, and constraints weighing on, the parties.

Management Buy-Outs and Leveraged Buy-Outs

[167] These transactions are becoming more common in Belgium. However, the main obstacle to them stems from section 629 of the Companies Code, incorporated into Belgian law pursuant to the Second Directive of the EC Council, whereby a société anonyme/naamloze vennootschap (public limited liability company) can only advance funds or grant loans or provide security for the acquisition of its own shares or assets by a third party under particular conditions. Like Article 23 of the Second Directive, section 629(2) of the Companies Code provides for derogations from these restrictions, provided that the sums used for this transaction are distributable according to section 617 of the Companies Code, i.e.: (i) advances, loans or securities granted to employees of the company or of a related company for the acquisition of their shares or certificates; (ii) advances, loans or securities granted to banks and other financial institutions within the framework of their normal business activities, on condition that the transactions take place under normal market conditions, governed by the Act of 25 April 2014 on the statute and regulation on financial institutions; and (iii) advances, loans or securities granted to companies of which at least the half of the voting rights are held by the employees of the company for the acquisition by these companies of the company's shares or certificates.

[168] Section 629 of the Companies Code deals with advances, loans or securities fronted by the company. Not all forms of financial assistance by the company being purchased are therefore governed by this section. Various measures aimed at reducing the cost of management buy-outs (e.g., distribution of reserves or reduction of capital) are not covered by this provision. Furthermore, the provision does not apply to every form of company, but only to sociétés anonymes/naamloze vennootschappen.

[169] Difficulties arising under section 629 of the Companies Code can result in creditors provisionally accepting a pledge of the company's shares, accompanied by certain restrictions such as a prohibition on the company entering into any further loan agreements, grant of a lease over a building, declaring dividends, giving guarantees to third parties, or mortgaging specific assets (including the business itself). In addition, for those companies not covered by section 629 of the Companies Code, it may be argued that granting of such charges would be *ultra vires,* though such problems could be resolved by a rather wide interpretation of the 'best interests of the company'.

[170] Generally speaking, in the case of transfers of a controlling interest, the presence of minority shareholders often constitutes an obstacle to certain transactions intended to take place once the transfer has been consummated. Often, the entire cash flow generated by the offeree company is in fact required to pay off loans taken out by the managers. In addition, subsequent restructuring operations (e.g., a merger with the purchasing company or the sale of certain assets), use of the company's credit, decisions to declare dividends or, more generally, intentions to adopt some long-term policy, could be sources of permanent conflict with minority shareholders, even if the interests of the company, widely construed, in principle prevailed over the personal interests of the shareholders. The problem derives from the fact that there are no specific mechanisms under Belgian company law permitting such minority shareholders to be bought out or to carry out a 'cash-out merger'.

Strategic Alliances

[171] Certain large Belgian companies have entered into alliances with foreign companies. The possibility of putting together a contractual group, such as is envisaged by the draft of the Ninth Directive, is not available under Belgian law and, more particularly, the concept of unitary management of the activities of two companies, with neither becoming the subsidiary of the other, raises difficult problems.

[172] The most advanced integration techniques normally take the form of bringing together jointly owned subsidiaries and the creation of consultative committees for the development of strategy and coordination.

Pooling

[173] Pooling is where two or more companies jointly pool all or part of their activities in order to share the resulting profits and losses. They often take the form of a joint venture. The best-known example of dividend pooling is Unilever.

[174] Integrated pooling of profits and assets can be achieved using two or more companies while providing for uniformity in their administration by ensuring the equal or identical composition of the management bodies. A long-standing example is the Agfa-Gevaert grouping of companies, but it is not the only one. This formula, which translates into a highly integrated rapprochement, has inspired the former Fortis group, bringing together the Belgian company A.G. and the Dutch company Amev, as well as the Dexia operation, bringing together the Crédit Communal de Belgique and the Crédit Local de France. The holding structure set up allows virtually the entire assets and liabilities of the companies in question to be brought under one roof within two national entities, of which each of the two top holding companies directly or indirectly holds 50%.

Share-Twinning

[175] Share-twinning is a further alternative. Under this formula, the shares issued by two or more public limited liability companies are institutionally linked so that each shareholder is necessarily a shareholder of all the other issuing companies. An old example is Eurotunnel, where France-Manche SA and The Channel Group Ltd, French and English companies, respectively, were awarded the licence to operate the Channel Tunnel. They were constituted to this effect and set up the Eurotunnel joint venture between themselves. The two companies have one board of directors and one management made up of the same individuals. Their shares are twinned and form indivisible units. Thus, each shareholder is perforce a shareholder of both companies, which present themselves as a single economic ensemble.

Joint Ownership Company and Temporary Company

[176] A joint ownership company (société interne/stille handelsvennootschap) is a commercial company that must satisfy the general characteristics of a company but is not endowed with legal personality. It is managed by at least one of the partners who is acting in its own name. It is completely transparent, both in this regard and from a commercial and fiscal viewpoint.

[177] A temporary company (*société momentanée/tijdelijke handels-vennootschap*) is not endowed with legal personality which is established by two or more partners for the purpose of carrying out one or several specific projects.

[178] Joint ownership companies and temporary companies are organized very liberally by the parties under the sole condition that they adhere to the essential characteristics relating to seeking to make a profit, the definition of corporate objects, the pooling of contributions (these can be limited to industry contributions), the non-ostensible nature of the company, the existence of at least two participating members and a managing member and the determination of internal relations. Moreover, they must of course be in line with public policy and mandatory laws. It follows that they may be tailor-made and used for all sorts of very different purposes.

[179] Joint ownership companies and temporary companies have been used on numerous occasions in Belgium to effect economic mergers, where a legal merger was not possible or not desirable. Here are a few examples:

- vehicles constituted for the purpose of issuing real estate certificates;
- the economic merger of joint municipal undertakings for the distribution of electricity, including the major provision of property installations;
- vehicles charged with construction projects and operations in the port of Antwerp or various other undertakings;
- complex economic groupings, including foreign companies and Belgian companies, in the area of major distribution;
- electricity, heat or nuclear production units and, more generally, industrial production units common to a number of companies;
- joint undertakings for services provided to a number of businesses.

Partnership

[180] The Companies Code, in its section 46, provides for the possibility to create a commercial company without personality, similar to a partnership, called a *société de droit commun/maatschap*, which need not necessarily present the characteristics of a joint ownership company or a joint venture. This development opens up new prospects for the creation of grouping or rapprochement instruments between undertakings without engaging in a merger.

EEIG and EIG

[181] European economic interest groupings (EEIGs) also constitute a method of cooperation between undertakings. They are subject to EEC Council Regulation 2137/85 of 25 July 1985. The measures for applying this regulation in national law took the form of an Act of 12 July 1989. At a Belgian domestic level, economic interest groupings (EIGs) in internal Belgian law are organized under Book XIV of the Companies Code. Both EEIGs and EIGs have legal personality. The object of these entities is to facilitate or develop the economic activities of their members and to improve or stimulate growth in the results of these activities, without making any profits for themselves, so that such entities have to remain ancillary to the activities of their members.

Joint Venture

[182] The English term 'joint venture' is used in Belgium to cover, in practice, highly varied forms of association in highly diverse areas. It has no precise legal definition. It generally means organization, in the form of a company or otherwise, of the relations between two or more undertakings, in order to set up and develop cooperation or a partial concentration among them in a given area of business. Setting up a 'joint venture' entails drawing up various contracts, over and above any deed of company incorporation, relating to financing, transfers of industrial property rights, administration of the cooperation or partial concentration agreement, the provision or transfer of staff and, possibly, relations between shareholders. In practice, joint ventures are often created to carry out specific projects.

SPECIFIC RULES RELATING TO SHARE OWNERSHIP

Implications of Different Levels of Investment

[183] The consequences of acquiring a stake in the capital of a Belgian public limited liability company (*société privée à responsabilité limitée/besloten vennootschap met beperke aansprakelijkheid*) vary, depending on the percentage obtained, i.e., more particularly:

(i) 1 share – Minority shareholders holding at least one share of a public limited liability company have, amongst others, the following rights:
- right to request the board of directors to convene a general shareholders' meeting in order to decide on the appointment of a statutory auditor, in the event no statutory auditor must be appointed pursuant to applicable laws (section 165 of the Companies Code);
- individual power of investigation and control in the event no statutory auditor has been appointed (section 166 of the Companies Code);
- right to be convened at and to participate in general shareholders' meetings (section 533 of the Companies Code);
- right to ask questions to the board of directors and to the statutory auditor at the occasion of general shareholders' meetings (section 540, Companies Code);
- right to vote at general shareholders' meetings (section 541 of the Companies Code);
- right to sign the minutes of the general shareholders' meetings (section 546 of the Companies Code);
- right to take knowledge of certain corporate documents, such as of the annual accounts and the management report (section 553 of the Companies Code);
- right to request the judicial winding-up of the company in the event the net assets have fallen below the minimum legally required capital (section 634 of the Companies Code);
- right to introduce a liability action against the directors of the dissolved company in the event of misconduct performed in the preparation and realization of the merger or of the demerger (section 687 of the Companies Code);
- right to introduce a liability action against the statutory auditor, auditor or accountant in the event of misconduct performed in the execution of its mandate within the framework of a merger or demerger (section 687 of the Companies Code);
- right to claim the annulment of the decision of the general shareholders' meetings (section 178 of the Companies Code);
- right to introduce, for valid grounds (*justes motifs/gegronde redenen*), a judicial action against other shareholders in view for these shareholders

to takeover all their shares, bonds or warrants (section 642 of the Companies Code).

(ii) 1% or EUR1 250 000 – Shareholders holding at least 1% or EUR1 250 000 of the share capital have the following rights:
- right to raise a minority action in the interest of the company pursuant to section 562 of the Companies Code, i.e., a legal action against the board of directors in cases where, regardless of the opposition of the minority, the majority shareholders have decided to exonerate and discharge the board from its liability for the foregoing year;
- right to apply to the commercial court for appointment of an expert to check the books and accounts of the company in the event the company's interests are, or are threatened to be, seriously prejudiced (sections 168 and 169 of the Companies Code).

(iii) 5% – Pursuant to the Act of 2 May 2007 and the Royal Decree of 14 February 2008 on the disclosure of substantial interests, acquisition or disposal of 5% of securities with voting rights of a Belgian listed company and of any tranche of 5% above that figure (which may be reduced to a minimum of 1% by the articles of association of the company in question) held by a shareholder or by shareholders acting in concert requires notification to the FSMA and the listed company within four business days as of such acquisition or disposal.

(iv) 10% – Section 606 of the Companies Code provides that a capital increase within the limits of the authorized capital, paid for by a contribution mainly in kind, is illegal if the subscribing shareholder already holds 10% or more of the capital.

(v) Although 10% constituted the maximum proportion a company may hold, directly or indirectly, in its own capital, either as a shareholder (section 620, Companies Code) or by way of a pledge (section 630), under pain of nullity of the shares concerned, the Royal Decree of 8 October 2008 raised this cap to 20%. Similarly, affiliate companies may not hold more than 10% of the capital of the parent company (section 631, Companies Code). Finally, the same limit applies to cross-holdings (section 632, Companies Code). Paradoxically, the Royal Decree of 8 October 2008 did not alter this 10% cap: the Directive of 6 September 2006 that this royal decree was intended to transpose, does not deal with the subject of cross-holdings.

(vi) 20% – The FSMA reserves the right to demand documents or additional information from major shareholders (section 23(2)(3°), Act of 2 May 2007).

(vii) 20% – Shareholders holding at least 20% of the share capital have the following rights:
- right to request the board of directors or the statutory auditor to call a general shareholders' meeting (section 532 of the Companies Code);
- right to block resolutions requiring an 80% majority, i.e., amendment of the company's objects (section 559 of the Companies Code).

(viii) Over 25% – A shareholder holding over 25% of the share capital may:
- block amendments to the articles of association, including increases in capital (section 558 of the Companies Code);
- decide on the winding-up of the company in the event the net assets have fallen below 75% of the share capital (section 633 of the Companies Code).

(ix) 30% – One or more shareholders together holding shares representing either 30% of the votes attached to all the existing shares or 20% if the company has issued shares not representing the share capital, or holding shares whose nominal or par value represents 30% of the company's capital, may apply to the president of the commercial court and, if serious and justified cause is shown, obtain a court injunction ordering:
- the defendant to transfer its shares to said shareholder or shareholders at a price fixed by the court (sections 636, Companies Code); or
- those exercising votes in a capacity other than as owners of shares to transfer their voting rights to the owner or owners of the shares in question (section 641, Companies Code).

(x) 30% – Pursuant to section 5 of the Act of 1 April 2007 on public takeover bids, any person who holds more than 30% of the securities with voting rights in the capital of a Belgian company admitted to trading on a regulated market or on a Multilateral Trading Facility (MTF) following an acquisition must inform the FSMA within two business days as of this acquisition and launch a public offer for all securities conferring access to voting rights.

(xi) over 50% – Shareholders having a majority in general shareholders' meetings can control the composition of the board of directors and the appointment of the statutory auditor; they can grant them the discharge; they may approve (or reject) the annual financial statements and pass resolutions for the allocation of profits. It should also be noted that the reduced taxation rates provided for under section 215 of the Income Tax Code 1992, which are available where the taxable income of the company does not exceed EUR322 500, do not apply where 50% or more of the capital is held by one or more companies, as opposed to individuals.

(xii) 75% – A majority of at least 75% is required in the general shareholders' meeting to adopt resolutions relating to:
- amendments to the articles of association, except particular amendments which require larger majorities (section 558 of the Companies Code);
- capital increase (section 581 of the Companies Code);
- limitation or cancellation of the preferential subscription rights in respect to capital increases and issuance of convertible bonds or warrants (section 596 of the Companies Code);
- the granting of special powers to the board of directors to increase the share capital by way of 'authorized capital' or to issue convertible bonds or warrants (sections 603 and 604 of the Companies Code);
- capital decrease (section 612 of the Companies Code);
- the repurchase by the company of the shares without voting right (section 626 of the Companies Code);
- the prorogation of the company incorporated for a definite duration (section 645(1) of the Companies Code);
- the winding-up of the company (section 645(2) of the Companies Code);
- the winding-up of the company in the event the net assets have fallen below the half of its share capital (section 633 of the Companies Code);
- the merger or demerger of the company (sections 699 and 736, Companies Code);

- the contribution of all the assets (*apport d'universalité/inbreng van een algemeenheid*) of the company to another company (section 761, Companies Code).
- All the above resolutions require a particular attendance quorum at the general shareholders' meeting, i.e., attendance of the shareholders representing at least 50% of the share capital, failing which a second meeting must be convened -which can take decisions regardless the portion of the share capital represented.

(xiii) 80% – A majority of over 80% is necessary to:
- amend the company's objects (section 559, Companies Code);
- convert the company into another form of company with a limited liability regime (section 781 of the Companies Code).

(xiv) 90% – A takeover bid that has resulted in such a majority holding must be reopened (section 35 of the Royal Decree of 27 April 2007 on takeover bids).

(xv) If a public limited liability company (SA/NV) already owns at least 90%, but not all, of the shares of the target company, the shareholders' meeting does not have to approve the merger if certain conditions are met (section 699(6) of the Companies Code).

(xvi) 95% – Squeeze-out: any person who, acting alone or in concert with others, holds 95% of the shares conferring voting rights may acquire the remaining shares. If the company has made or makes public calls on investors, such acquisition must result from a takeover bid. At the outcome of the procedure, the shares not presented, whether or not the owner has manifested itself, are deemed transferred by operation of law upon deposit of the price. If the company did not or does not make public calls on investors, any such person may offer to buy out the remaining shareholders. At the outcome of the procedure, the shares not presented are deemed to have been transferred by operation of law upon deposit of the price, except for those shares whose owner has intimated expressly in writing that he or she refuses to dispose thereof. Those shares are not transferred but are then converted into registered shares (section 513 of the Companies Code).

(xvii) 100% – The unanimity of the shareholders is required for the adoption of the following resolutions:
- derogation from the requirement to propose to all shareholders or securities holders to acquire their shares or securities under the same conditions in the event of share buy-backs (section 620 § 1 (5°) of the Companies Code);
- conversion of the company (i) into a company with an unlimited liability regime, or (ii) if the company does not exist for at least two years or (iii) if the articles of association prohibit the conversion of the company (section 781, §5 of the Companies Code);
- demerger of the company in the event the shares of the acquiring company are not distributed *prorata* the rights of the shareholders in the share capital of the demerged company (section 736, §5 of the Companies Code);
- written resolutions (section 536 of the Companies Code).

A public limited liability company *(société anonyme/naamloze vennootschap)* must have a minimum of two bona fide shareholders. However, a public company limited by shares entirely held by one shareholder only is not automatically wound up. Within a period of one year, this situation must be regularized by:

- a second bona fide shareholder taking a shareholding in that company; or
- conversion of the company into a one-man private company limited by shares (société unipersonnelle/eenpersoonsvennootschap); or
- winding-up of the company.

If none of these solutions has been implemented within one year, the sole shareholder is deemed to be wholly liable for all the debts of the company that arise after the shares came into his hands, and until one of the three solutions referred to above has been effected.

Limitation on Voting Powers

[184] An important provision is to be found in section 544 of the Companies Code. The previous wording of this section provided for a limitation on the voting powers of shareholders holding more than 20% of the share capital in a Belgian company. Under the old provision, no shareholder could vote, either in his or her own name or by proxy, so as to cast a total number of votes exceeding one-fifth of the number of votes attributable to all outstanding shares and two-fifths of the votes attaching to the shares actually represented at the meeting. The significance of this provision was that it led to a shareholder who held a majority in number of the shares nevertheless being prevented from exercising full voting powers, such that the shareholder could be in a minority position if faced with a group of minority shareholders acting in concert who together owned more than 20% of the capital. For this reason, large shareholders frequently distributed shares among various companies or persons within their own group, in order to avoid any such limitation on their voting rights. As a result of the amendment of 18 July 1991, this limitation on voting powers became optional and is no longer mandatory. It will apply only to companies whose articles of association contain a provision stating that such a limitation is to apply. Inclusion of this clause in articles of association is now extremely rare.

Special Majority Rules: Shareholders' Agreements

[185] The articles of association of Belgian companies may deviate from certain voting rules. Special majorities, higher than those envisaged by the Companies Code, may be stipulated for passing resolutions relating to specific issues. Moreover, adequate representation of the various groups of shareholders at board level may be achieved either by means of a shareholders' agreement, taking the matter outside the articles of association, or preferably by inserting appropriate clauses into the articles of association, including the creation of various classes of shares. The validity of shareholders' agreements is subject to the provisions of section 510 and section 551 of the Companies Code. The first of these sections limits shareholders' agreements limiting the transferability of shares, to a maximum duration which must be fixed in advance and provides that any such shareholders' agreement must, at all times, be in the 'best interests of the company'.

[186] Section 551 of the Companies Code furthermore renders null and void any agreement that (a) is in breach of the Companies Code or of the 'best interests of the company' or (b) obliges any shareholder to vote in accordance with directives given by the company or a subsidiary, or (c) contains an undertaking by the shareholder not to reject a proposal from the company. According to section 510 of the Companies Code, restrictions on the transferability of shares in the case of approval clauses or pre-emption agreements entailing a right of first refusal must be limited to six months from the request to sell or for approval of the sale.

COMMON FINANCING METHODS

[187] An acquisition may generally be paid for in a number of ways, either by a cash payment, payment in shares or the issue of debentures (convertible or otherwise), and the financing of the transaction will generally depend upon the method of payment used. However, it would appear that, although in fact acquisitions for cash used to be the most common, whether carried out by way of a takeover bid or by way of a private acquisition agreement, exchanges of shares are now frequent. An exchange of shares will take place either where the aim of the parties is to acquire interlocking interests or where the intention is to integrate the shareholders of the offeree company into a wider group.

[188] The finance sought usually takes the form of bank loans, which may be refinanced on the debenture markets. As in many countries, the choice of financing methods will also be influenced by the deductibility of interest for tax purposes.

Shares

[189] Increases in share capital have now become more common than in the past. If shares are intended to finance an acquisition or a public offer to exchange shares of one company for the shares of another, the problems which arise are those generally encountered in any placement of shares on the market, and the regulations relating to public offers will apply.

[190] If the shares are issued in the context of an amalgamation of undertakings, e.g., in exchange for part of a business or in exchange for other shares, the problems that arise are not specific to mergers and acquisitions but are those generally encountered in the case of contributions in kind or contracts of exchange. In particular, the assets or shares concerned will have to be valued by the statutory auditor of the company concerned or, if no statutory auditor has been appointed, by a chartered auditor (reviseur/revisor).

[191] The Companies Code provide that an increase in capital may be resolved by the board of directors but only within certain limits fixed by resolution of the general meeting of shareholders. Such a resolution may authorize the board of directors to effect one or more increases of capital, as and when it thinks fit, within a maximum of five years and up to a ceiling established by the general meeting.

[192] The Act of 25 April 2014 on the regulation and control of financial institutions strictly limits the possibility for banks and other financial institutions to hold shares in others companies. This is only allowed for certain services to clients within certain limits. Proprietary trading is forbidden.

Loan Stock, Convertible Loan Stock and Warrants

[193] Belgian public limited liability companies (sociétés anonymes/naamloze vennootschappen) may issue debentures, and the rights of the debenture holders are laid down in certain provisions of the Companies Code. However, major issues of bonds or notes are, primarily for tax reasons, often effected through a subsidiary incorporated in a country where no withholding tax is payable on interest.

[194] Similarly, the Companies Code provides that sociétés anonymes/naamloze vennootschappen may issue convertible debentures or debentures with a right of subscription attached in the form of a special coupon known as a warrant. Subscription is only valid for shares; shares may only be subscribed in cash. The period within which conversion or subscription must take place is limited to a maximum of ten years and the decision to issue may be taken by the shareholders' meeting or by the board of directors, within the limits of the authorized capital. Finally, the rights of preference shares may be overridden if this is justified in the interests of the company. In that case, however, the warrant must be limited to five years. Conditions of issue providing for compulsory exercise of the warrant are void.

BELGIAN MERGER CONTROL LAW AND PRACTICE

Regulatory Framework

[195] As from 3 April 2013, the bulk of the Belgian rules governing this area are contained in Book IV of the new 'CEL' covering competition law.

[196] At a European Union level, Articles 101 and 102 of the Treaty on the Functioning of the European Union ('TFEU') govern the protection of competition. However, the TFEU does not contain any rules governing the control of concentrations. The EU merger control rules are enacted in Regulation 139/2004 of the Council of 20 January 2004 on the control of concentrations between undertakings ('Regulation 139/2004').

[197] As will be explained below, the two regimes are, in essence, mutually exclusive in their application.

The Administrative Authorities

[198] The reformed Belgian competition authority ('BCA') is responsible for the enforcement of the competition law provisions in the CEL. The BCA is an independent body composed of a President, the Competition College that is presided by the President, the College of the Competition Prosecutors and a Management

Committee. The BCA has no jurisdiction in relation to unfair competition or acts contrary to fair commercial practices, which are both regulated by Book VI of the CEL and fall within the exclusive jurisdiction of the courts.

[199] The Competition College is the decision-making body within the BCA, and its powers include issuing clearance decisions in merger investigations. The Competition College is assembled on a case-by-case basis by the President of the BCA and consists of the President or Assessor-Vice President and two assessors.

[200] The Management Committee is the body within the BCA that is entrusted with the daily management and the policy making of the BCA. The Management Committee's powers include deciding on the enforcement priorities of the BCA and issuing guidelines in relation to the application of the competition rules. The Management Committee consists of the President, the Competition Prosecutor General, the Director of economic studies and the Director of legal studies.

[201] The College of Competition Prosecutors, which is headed by the Competition Prosecutor General, conducts all investigations and presents its case to the Competition College, which then takes a decision on the case. However, in simplified merger filings, the members of the College of Competition Prosecutors can also issue decisions. The powers of the Competition Prosecutor General include but are not limited to:

- the management of the Competition College and the coordination of the investigations;
- receiving notifications of concentrations;
- the execution of the decisions taken by the Competition College or the judgments of the Brussels Court of Appeal in competition cases;
- appointing a Competition Prosecutor to each individual case who will be in charge of leading the investigation.

[202] The Competition College is assisted by the registry which carries out the requisite administrative tasks and is responsible for receiving merger notifications and other submissions.

Ambit of Merger Control Legislation

[203] The control of concentrations is governed at an EU level, by Regulation 139/2004, at Belgian level, by Book IV of the CEL.

[204] Regulation 139/2004 in principle only applies to concentrations with an EU dimension. The European Commission has exclusive jurisdiction to examine concentrations with an EU dimension (i.e., concentrations that meet certain turnover thresholds, *see* below). National laws can only apply to the extent the operation is not subject to Regulation 139/2004. To delimit its ambit, Regulation 139/2004 thus defines the notions of concentration and EU dimension.

[205] Concentrations falling under Regulation 139/2004 (which has been transposed into Belgian law) concern the following categories of operations:

- the merger of two previously independent undertakings;

- acquisition of direct or indirect control of another undertaking;
- creation of a full-function joint venture to permanently carry on independent business activities.

[206] In this regard, the notion of control is central to the extent that a concentration is only deemed to arise if a permanent change in control would result from one of these operations. Control has to be interpreted as the possibility of exercising 'decisive influence' over an undertaking on the basis of rights, contracts or other means. This can be on a legal basis, but also on a de facto basis. Control can also be positive, negative, sole or joint.

[207] Furthermore, as stated above, in order to be subject to Regulation 139/2004, the concentration must have an EU dimension. The settled criterion for assessing this is the turnover of the parties to the transaction.

[208] The system of thresholds set up by the regulation can be summarized as follows:

- To have a Union dimension, the concentration must concern undertakings whose total worldwide turnover is greater than EUR5 bn and where the total turnover realized individually in the European Union by at least two of these undertakings is greater than EUR250 mn.
- Nonetheless, if the above criteria are not met, Regulation 139/2004 also applies to smaller concentrations that have an impact in at least three Member States. These concentrations are caught by Regulation 139/2004 if the total worldwide turnover of all parties exceeds EUR2.5 b, the total European Union-wide turnover of each of at least two parties exceeds EUR100 mn, in each of at least three Member States, the total turnover of all the parties exceeds EUR100 mn, and in these three Member States, the turnover of each of at least two parties exceeds EUR25 mn.
- For both of these turnover thresholds, even if the above criteria are met, the concentration will not have an EU dimension if each of the undertakings realizes more than two-thirds of its turnover in a single Member State.

[209] In principle, concentrations that do not exceed these thresholds are governed by national competition law, whilst concentrations that meet the above thresholds have an EU dimension, and thus fall within the exclusive jurisdiction of the European Commission. However, as Regulation 139/2004 foresees in a system of referrals to ensure that a concentration is examined by the authority best placed to conduct the assessment, a concentration that does have a Union dimension may nevertheless be subject to control at a national level. The national competition authority (Article 9 Regulation 139/2004) or the merging parties (Article 4(4) Regulation 139/2004) can request that a concentration that meets the notification thresholds as set out in Regulation 139/2004 is reviewed – in whole or in part – by the national competition authority. Conversely, a control referral can be made by a Member State to the European Commission if trade between Member States is affected even where the concentration does not present any EU dimension (Articles 4(5) and 22 Regulation 139/2004). Partial referrals of certain elements of a transaction are also possible.

[210] Chapter 2 of Book IV of the CEL sets out the Belgian rules on concentration control. It sets forth the same definition as is contained in Regulation 139/2004.

Therefore, subject to the exceptions described above, a concentration that does not have a Union dimension can be subject to concentration control in Belgium. However, in order to be notifiable in Belgium, the concentration would still have meet the thresholds set out in Article IV.7. of the CEL. The thresholds are the following:

- the total turnover of the parties is greater than EUR100 mn in Belgium;
- at least of the parties have individually generated turnover greater than EUR40 mn in Belgium.

Obligation to Notify

Concentrations Subject to Control by the European Commission

[211] Regulation 139/2004 gives the parties the possibility to notify their concentration even before any agreement has been entered into. In order to do so, the undertakings concerned must demonstrate to the European Commission their good faith intention to conclude an agreement. In case of a public bid, There needs to be a public announcement of such bid.

[212] If the notification is incomplete, it will only be effective as from the date of receipt of the missing information by the European Commission.

[213] A concentration with an EU dimension may not be implemented until it has been notified and declared by the European Commission to be compatible with the internal market. The European Commission can grant a derogation from this suspension obligation if it is confirmed that the detriment to the notifying parties or to a third party resulting from the suspension exceeds the threats to competition posed by the transaction. Such derogation cannot be obtained by demonstrating hypothetical threats.

Concentrations Subject to Control by the Belgian Competition Authority

[214] Undertakings must notify their concentration before it is implemented and after signature of the agreement, publication of the takeover or tender bid, or acquisition of a controlling holding. The parties can also notify a draft agreement, provided they expressly declare that they have the intention of entering into an agreement that does not significantly differ from the draft as notified as regards the relevant points of competition law. In the case of a takeover or tender bid, the parties may also notify a draft where they have publicly announced their intention of submitting such a bid.

[215] The undertakings concerned may not implement the concentration until the Competition College has issued a decision on its compatibility. However, the President may at any time grant a derogation from this notification obligation on request by the parties.

Investigation: Commencement of the Administrative Procedure

Concentrations Subject to Control by the European Commission

[216] Once the European Commission receives notification of a concentration, its task is to verify the facts contained in the notification. In doing so, the European Commission has certain powers of investigation, such as the right to demand information from the parties to the concentration, from third parties or from Member States (Article 11, Regulation 139/2004). The European Commission may also gain access to the undertaking's premises, inspect the books and other documents relating to the business, request copies and ask the staff and representatives for explanations as to the facts and documents relating to the subject matter being inspected if it suspects the parties to have implemented the transaction prior to approval (this happens only very rarely). Third parties with sufficient interest may ask the European Commission to be heard.

[217] In addition, the European Commission must conduct the procedure in close and constant cooperation with the competent authorities in the Member States, which may make observations on the procedure. The European Commission shall send copies of the notifications to the competent authorities within three days from the day they were received by the European Commission. The European Commission will also as soon as possible hand over important documents that are sent to it together with the documents issued by it.

Concentrations Subject to Control by the Belgian Competition Authority

[218] The Competition Prosecutor appointed by the Competition Prosecutor General shall initiate a 'Phase I' investigation upon receipt of the notification or, if the information to be provided was incomplete, upon receipt of the complete information. The Competition Prosecutor will send a copy of the notification of the concentration, without any delay, to the President, who then will appoint the Competition College that will be deciding on the case. The Competition Prosecutor, who is in charge of the daily management of an investigation, can assign investigative duties to the members of the staff of the investigation service.

[219] The notifying parties may request application of the simplified procedure. In order to obtain a clearance decision through the simplified procedure, the concentration must meet certain condition as set out in a guidance document of the BCA. According to this guidance document concentrations where the undertakings concerned jointly control less than 25% of the market are eligible for the simplified procedure.

[220] If the Competition Prosecutor that is investigating the concentration decides that the conditions for the application of the simplified procedure are satisfied, and that there aren't any objections to the notified concentration, this shall be communicated to the notifying parties in writing with fifteen working days. Simultaneously, the Competition Prosecutor shall transmit a copy of that letter to the registry of the BCA for publication. According to Article IV.64 §4 CEL, this decision of the Competition Prosecutor shall be regarded as a decision of the Competition College.

[221] In the event of a regular Phase I procedure, the Competition Prosecutor must lodge a reasoned draft decision together with the underlying case file with the President within twenty-five working days following the day the notification was received. This twenty-five working day period can be extended with five working days when commitments have been presented. The reasoned draft decision must contain the investigation report and a proposed decision; it is accompanied by the investigation dossier and an inventory of the documents contained therein. This inventory sets forth whether the documents are confidential in relation to parties inspecting the dossier. This draft decision is also transmitted to the notifying parties.

[222] The Competition College also plays an investigatory role to the extent that it examines each case at the hearing. The hearing is held at least ten working days after the draft decision is sent to the notifying parties. The parties may submit their written observations no later than the day preceding the hearing and provide the Competition Prosecutor with a copy. Where it considers it to be necessary, the Competition College can also hear any other natural or legal persons or any third person that demonstrates a sufficient interest.

Decision and Second Phase of the Investigation

Concentrations Subject to Control by the European Commission

[223] Within twenty-five working days following the effective date of notification, the European Commission must issue a decision as to whether the concentration is compatible with the internal market. The European Commission authorizes the operation if it does not significantly hinder competition in the internal market. In a Phase I investigation this can be extended to thirty-five working days if remedies are offered to the parties.

[224] Following the first phase of the procedure, the European Commission will decide that:

- the concentration does not fall under Regulation 139/2004;
- the concentration is compatible with the internal market;
- the concentration is compatible with the internal market provided certain conditions are met; or
- there are serious doubts as to the concentration's compatibility with the internal market, and embark upon the Phase II procedure.

[225] If the European Commission opens a Phase II investigation it must take a decision within ninety working days (as various extensions are possible, this period may in practice be longer) declaring that:

- the concentration is compatible with the internal market;
- the concentration is compatible with the internal market provided certain conditions are met; or
- the concentration is not compatible with the internal market.

Concentrations Subject to Control by the Belgian Competition Authority

[226] The Competition College must take a decision within forty working days of the day following the date of notification. This period is extended by fifteen working days where the undertakings present commitments for the purpose of rendering the concentration admissible.

[227] The Competition College's decision is based on the draft decision and particularly takes account of the necessity of preserving and developing effective competition, the possible choices of suppliers and users, and the interests of consumers.

[228] It declares concentrations to be admissible where they do not significantly hinder effective competition, especially by creating or reinforcing a dominant position.

[229] Where the undertakings together control less than 25% of the market, the Competition College must declare the operation to be admissible. If it proves necessary, the undertakings may submit commitments to assure that the concentration will be authorized. These commitments consist of conditions and burdens that the undertakings promise to abide by and that guarantee that the operations will not have any detrimental effect from a competition viewpoint.

[230] In the case of serious doubts as to the admissibility of the operation, the Competition College will embark a Phase II investigation which lasts sixty working days. This period is extended by a maximum of twenty working days if the undertakings involved propose commitments. This period may only be extended on the express request of the parties and for such period as they propose. The Competition College asks the Competition Prosecutor to submit to a draft decision within thirty working days following the decision to initiate the Phase II investigation. Subsequently a hearing is held and the Competition College will either declare the operation to be inadmissible or admissible, with or without conditions being attached.

[231] Please note that for Belgian merger control purposes, Saturdays are counted as working days. However, a legislative proposal has been submitted to exclude Saturdays as a working days for merger control purposes.

Penalties

Concentrations Subject to Control by the European Commission

[232] The Commission may impose:

(1) Periodic penalty payments of up to 5% of the total average daily turnover of the undertaking or association of undertakings concerned per working day of delay as from such date as it shall fix in its decision in order to oblige them to:
- (i) furnish certain information in a complete and accurate manner;
- (ii) undergo an investigation as ordered by way of a decision;
- (iii) comply with a burden imposed by way of a decision;
- (iv) take measures ordered by way of a decision;

2. fines of up to 1% of the total worldwide turnover of the undertaking where, wilfully or negligently:
   (i) they give inaccurate or misleading details in relation to a notification or request for information;
   (ii) they provide information in an incomplete manner;
   (iii) they fail to provide information within the time allowed;
   (iv) they make an incomplete presentation of the books or other business documents required in connection with investigations or fail to submit to an investigation ordered by way of a consequential decision;
   (v) in response to a question asked in connection with an investigation, they provide an inaccurate or misleading answer, fail within the time allowed by the Commission to rectify an inaccurate, incomplete or misleading answer provided by a member of staff, or omit or refuse to provide a complete answer in relation to the subject matter and purpose of an investigation; or
   (vi) seals affixed by the agents of the Commission or authorized persons accompanying them are broken;
3. fines of up to 10% of total worldwide turnover where undertakings, wilfully or negligently:
   (i) fail to notify a concentration before its implementation, unless they were expressly authorized to do so;
   (ii) implement a concentration before it is authorized;
   (iii) implement a concentration declared to be incompatible with the internal market; or
   (iv) they contravene a condition or burden that has been laid down.

Concentrations Subject to Control by the Belgian Competition Authority

[233] The Competition College may impose:

4. fines of up to 5% of average daily turnover for undertakings that fail to adhere to prohibition decisions or decisions allowing concentrations subject to conditions;
5. fines of up to 1% of turnover on undertakings that fail to notify a concentration falling within the ambit of Book IV of the CEL;
6. fines of up to 1% of turnover where, wilfully or negligently:
   (i) they give inaccurate or misleading details in connection with a notification or request for information;
   (ii) they provide incomplete information;
   (iii) they fail to provide information within the time allowed;
   (iv) they hinder or prevent investigations or general or sectoral inquiries;
7. fines of up to 10% of turnover where undertakings implement a concentration before it qualifies as admissible or fail to abide by prohibition decisions or decisions whereby a concentration is allowed subject to conditions.

Judicial Review

Appealing Decisions Rendered by the European Commission

[234] The European Commission's decision that a concentration is incompatible with the internal market may be appealed to the General Court. Also decisions to carry out an investigation or a decision in which the European Commission fixes a fine or periodic penalty payments may be appealed to the General Court. In this latter case, the General Court may set aside, reduce or increase the fine or coercive penalty imposed. Subsequently judgments of the General Court can be appealed to the European Court of Justice.

Appealing Decisions Rendered by the Belgian Competition Council

[235] The decisions of the Competition College (as well as the tacit decisions of the permissibility of concentrations) may be appealed before the Brussels Court of Appeal within thirty days after notification of the decision of the Competition College. Also investigative measures taken by the College of Competition Prosecutors, can be appealed to the Brussels Court of Appeal.

[236] Each person who has asked to be heard during the session can lodge an appeal before the Brussels Court of Appeal at the latest thirty days after notification of the decision. The competent Minister can also lodge an appeal without having to show a sufficient interest, and without being heard during the hearing sessions of the Competition College.

[237] Decisions whereby a concentration falls within the scope of application the CEL and those which provide for the supplementary investigation procedure to be initiated shall not be considered as final decisions within the framework of this appeal procedure.

TAXATION ASPECTS

Belgian Corporation Tax System

Taxation of Profits

[238] Any legal entity which has been duly incorporated, has legal personality and carries on a business is deemed to be a company for income tax purposes (sections 2, 5° of the Income Tax Code 1992 ('ITC92'). If the company has established its registered office, its principal place of business or the seat of its management in Belgium, it will in principle be subject to Belgian corporate income tax (corporation tax). If that place is located outside Belgium, the company may, depending on the circumstances, have some its income be subject to non-resident corporate income tax (non-resident corporation tax).

[239] The taxable base of entities that are subject to corporate income tax is, as a rule, composed of its worldwide income, less fiscally allowable deductions. Belgian tax law foresees however also alternative corporate tax regimes for certain types of entities, such as pension funds, regulated real estate companies, etc. that are not profit-based. The taxable base of such entities is generally composed of non-deductible items and received abnormal or benevolent advantages.

[240] The standard corporation tax rate is 33.99%, i.e., 33% as a basic rate, to which a 3% crisis surcharge calculated on the basis rate is added. The effective corporation tax rate can be significantly lowered as a result of application of a number of tax deductions that may be available.

[241] The nominal flat rate will in principle always be applicable where the company's profits exceed EUR322 500 (section 215, ITC92). However, if the amount of the company's taxable profits does not exceed EUR322 500, then, under certain conditions, the following rates may apply:

- 24.98% (24.25% plus the 3% crisis surcharge calculated on the basis rate) on the first EUR25 000;
- 31.93% (31.00% plus the 3% crisis surcharge calculated on the basis rate) on the band up to EUR90 000;
- 35.54% (34.50% plus the 3% crisis surcharge calculated on the basis rate) on the band up to EUR322 500.

[242] The cumulative conditions which should be fulfilled in order to apply these reduced corporation tax rates are as follows:

(i) the company does not hold an investment value in shares representing over 50% of its revalued paid-up capital or its paid-up capital plus taxable reserves and recorded capital gains;
(ii) the shares of the company are not held by one or more other companies (as opposed to individuals) to the extent of 50% or more;
(iii) dividend distributions by the company do not amount to over 13% of the paid-up capital;
(iv) at least one of the company's officers (dirigeants d'entreprise/ bedrijfsleiders) receive emoluments of at least EUR36 000 per annum or at least an amount equal to the taxable income of the company if that amount is lower; the company;
(v) may not be a collective investment company.

Taxation of Distributed Dividends

[243] For Belgian corporation tax purposes, distributed dividends are part of the taxable profit of the taxable year in which the distribution takes place (section 185, first paragraph, ITC92). Hence, the amount of dividends distributed will be subject to the applicable corporation tax rate.

[244] A Belgian-resident company distributing dividends will in principle have to deduct dividend withholding tax at source. Withholding tax will be due at the time when the dividend is attributed or is made available for payment (section 267, first paragraph, ITC92). Within fifteen days following the day of attribution or the day the dividend is made available for payment, the applicable withholding tax should be paid to the Belgian treasury (section 412, first paragraph, ITC92). Furthermore, within the same fifteen-day period, a withholding tax return should be filed with the relevant Belgian income tax office.

[245] The normal withholding tax rate applicable to dividends is in principle 27%. However, under certain conditions, a reduced rate or exemption may be applicable. The withholding tax rate applicable to redemption and liquidation payments is 27%.

[246] Reduced tax rates may apply to the distribution of dividends (other than share buybacks or liquidation dividends) related to newly registered shares that were issued after 1 July 2013. These reduced rates apply provided that the following conditions are satisfied (section 269, second paragraph, ITC92):

- the new shares have been issued in exchange for a new cash contribution;
- these newly issued shares are registered shares;
- the company receiving the contribution qualifies as a small company in the sense of section 15 of the Companies Code;
- the newly issued shares are fully paid-up and are not preference shares; and
- the shareholder has, at all times since the contribution, retained full ownership of the registered shares (certain exceptions relax this retention requirement).
- The applicable reduced rate will be 20% for distributions made in respect of the profits generated during the second year following the contribution. Said reduced rate will be set at 15% for distributions made in respect of the profits generated during the third year following the contribution or during any year thereafter.

[247] Companies qualifying as small companies in the sense of section 15 of the Companies Code may set up a liquidation reserve in order to be able to distribute dividends at a reduced rate (sections 184*quater* and 171, 3° *septies* ITC92). This reserve can be formed through a requalification of the profits after tax as a liquidation reserve. This requalification is subject to a withholding tax of 10%. If the liquidation reserve is distributed before the company is liquidated or within five years after the creation of the reserve, an additional withholding tax of 17% will be due (effectively bringing the total tax to 27%). If the distribution takes place after more than five years as from the creation of the reserve, a withholding tax of 5% will be due (effectively bringing the total tax to 15%). No withholding tax is due if the liquidation reserve is distributed upon the liquidation of the company.

[248] In addition, dividend distributions made to a parent company established in the EU or in a country with which Belgium has concluded an agreement containing an exchange of information clause, may benefit from a withholding tax exemption, provided that the following conditions are met: (section 106, fifth and sixth paragraphs, Royal Decree implementing the ITC92 ('RD/ITC92'):

(i) both the distributing company and the company receiving the dividends qualify as 'companies of a Member State', which requires that they should:
   - be incorporated under one of the legal forms mentioned in the annex to the Parent-Subsidiary Directive or a similar legal form in case of a treaty

country. From a Belgian point of view, all legal forms of commercial companies qualify;

- have their residence for income tax purposes in an EU Member State or in a tax treaty country under that country's domestic tax law and under the terms of the double taxation treaties concluded by that country with third party States; and
- be subject to corporate income tax or to a similar tax in its country of residence without benefiting from a regime that deviates from the normal tax regime.

(ii) the parent company holds (or commits to hold) a minimum holding of 10% of the share capital of the Belgian distributing company; for an uninterrupted period of at least twelve months. Should this minimum holding condition not yet have been fulfilled at the time of payment or attribution of the dividend, then a certified commitment by the company receiving the dividend to fulfil the holding requirement will be sufficient to benefit from the withholding tax exemption. In that case, upon distribution, an amount equal to the withholding tax that would otherwise be due has to be set aside in a blocked reserve account for the remainder of the holding period. Once the holding period has actually elapsed, the funds can be transferred to the company receiving the dividend.

Dividend distributions made to non-resident companies that do not fulfil all the conditions under section 106, fifth and sixth paragraphs, RD/ITC92,, may still possibly be subject to reduced rates or to a zero rate under a double taxation treaty concluded by Belgium

[249] . Belgium has signed such treaties with more than ninety countries.

[250] For Belgian-resident corporate shareholders, Belgian withholding tax deducted at source is treated as an advance payment to be credited against final corporation tax due. Moreover, any excess will in principle be refundable. Crediting the withholding tax against Belgian corporation tax liability is nevertheless subject to two conditions (sections 281 and 282, ITC92):

(i) the company must have full legal ownership of the shares at the time the dividend is attributed or made available for payment; and

(ii) the attribution of the dividend or making it available for payment may not result in impairment of, or a capital loss on, the shares. This second condition does not apply where the company can evidence that it has had full legal ownership of the shares for an uninterrupted period of twelve months prior to attribution of the dividend or that, during that same period, the shares were not in the full legal ownership of a taxpayer who is not either a Belgian-resident company or a non-resident company that invested the shares continually in a Belgian establishment.

[251] For non-resident companies, the Belgian withholding tax deducted will in principle be the final tax due in Belgium. However, if the non-resident shareholder has invested his shares in a Belgian permanent establishment, then he will be subject to non-resident corporation tax. If the shares have indeed been so invested, the dividends will have to be reported in a non-resident income tax return and will be subject to non-resident corporation tax (subject to the participation exemption, see below) at the aforementioned standard rate of 33.99%, i.e., 33% plus 3% crisis surcharge calculated on the basic rate. Crediting the withholding tax deducted at source against the non-resident corporation tax due will be subject to the same conditions as apply to Belgian-resident companies.

Participation Exemption for Dividends Received

[252] Belgium has opted for the exemption method to avoid double taxation of domestic or foreign-source dividends received under its domestic tax legislation. This method is known as the dividend-received deduction or DRD (revenus définitivement taxés/definitief belaste inkomsten), allowing the Belgian-resident or non-resident corporation taxpayer to deduct from its tax base 95% of the amount of dividends received from its corporation tax basis (section 204, ITC92).

[253] The benefit of the DRD regime requires fulfilment of certain holding and 'subject to tax' conditions. The holding condition requires the following (section 202, second paragraph, ITC92):

(i) at the time at which the dividends are attributed or made available for payment, the Belgian parent company must have a minimum holding in its subsidiary's share capital of at least 10% or the acquisition value of the holding must be at least EUR2 500 000; and

(ii) the dividends received must derive from shares that have been or must be maintained in full legal ownership for an uninterrupted period for at least one year. If the parent company's holding has not been held for one year, the condition will nonetheless be deemed fulfilled for Belgian corporation tax return purposes, on a provisional basis, provided that the parent company declares that it intends to keep its holding for a minimum period of one year. If the parent company does not keep its holding for one year, then an additional tax return will have to be filed and any additional corporation tax liability that might be due will have to be paid.

[254] A dividend will only qualify under the DRD regime if the distributing company meets a subject-to-tax condition. The latter will not be met if the distributing company is not subject to Belgian corporation tax or to a foreign tax similar to Belgian corporation tax, or if it is established in a country where the ordinary tax regime is considerably more favourable than the regime applicable in Belgium. A tax regime will be considered more favourable than the regime applicable in Belgium, if its nominal tax rate or effective tax burden is below 15%. Companies established in an EU Member State are not affected by this condition.

[255] In addition, the DRD regime will not apply for dividends distributed by:

(i) a company receiving foreign non-dividend income that is subject to a separate tax regime deviating from the normal tax regime in the company's country of residence;

(ii) a company receiving income from a permanent establishment established outside of Belgium if, in the country where the establishment is located, said income is subject to a taxation regime that is substantially more advantageous than the Belgian regime. This exclusion will not apply if the income deriving from the permanent establishment is effectively taxed at a rate of 15% or higher or if the company and its permanent establishment are both established in an EU Member State; and

(iii) financing companies, treasury companies, investment companies, regulated real estate companies; dividends distributed by such entities may, however, under certain specific conditions, still be eligible for the DRD regime;

(iv) an intermediary company (re)distributing dividend income of which 10% or more is 'contaminated' pursuant to the above rules.

[256] Excess DRD generated by dividends received from companies established in the European Economic Area may in principle be carried forward to subsequent assessment years without limitation in time.

[257] The DRD regime will not be applicable to the amount of abnormal or gratuitous benefits received.

Tax Status of Interest

[258] Interest payable on loans taken out for the acquisition of Belgian or foreign shareholdings is fully deductible for Belgian corporation tax purposes. Such interest may be deducted either from dividends received or from the operating income of the Belgian recipient company.

[259] The deductibility of interest, combined with the 95% DRD, makes the Belgian holding regime exceptionally attractive in comparison with the tax regime applicable to similar types of companies in neighbouring countries, especially if the holding company concerned has operating activities or receives interest income. Although Belgian income tax law recognizes the concept of a 'company group' in certain specific areas, there is no income tax consolidation of profit and loss accounts within a group, or any system of group relief.

[260] Belgian-resident companies attributing interest or making interest available for payment, or any intervening financial institution established in Belgium, will in principle have to deduct withholding tax at source. The withholding tax rate applicable to interest payments is 27%. Furthermore, under certain conditions, a reduced withholding tax rate or a withholding tax exemption may be applicable.

[261] Under Belgian domestic legislation, no withholding tax will have to be deducted on the following interest payments:

(i) interest on loans or debt receivables attributed by companies subject to Belgian corporation tax or non-resident corporation tax that qualify as so-called professional investors (investisseurs professionnels/beroepsbeleggers) to qualifying credit institutions established in a country in the European Economic Area or a country with which Belgium has a bilateral double tax treaty (section 107, second paragraph (5°), RD/ITC92);

(ii) interest qualifying under the Interest & Royalties Directive of 3 June 2003 (Directive 2003/49/EC). The Belgian implementation of this directive provides that interest from bonds, cash certificates and similar securities, loans and debt receivables and, under certain conditions, real estate certificates is exempt from Belgian withholding tax subject to the following conditions (section 107, sixth paragraph, RD/ITC92):
   - the company receiving the interest should qualify as a 'company of a Member State', requiring it to be incorporated in one of the legal forms listed in the annex to the Interest & Royalties Directive. In the case of Belgium, any legal entity having its tax residence in Belgium qualifies as such. Moreover, it should have its residence for income tax purposes in an EU Member State and, under the terms of a double tax treaty signed with a third State, should not be considered to be tax resident outside the EU. Finally, it should be subject to Belgian corporation tax or the domestic corporation tax of the EU Member State where it is established;
   - the company receiving the interest and the debtor of the interest should both qualify as 'associated companies', which requires them to be established in the EU. This also requires one of the two associated companies to hold or have had a direct or indirect holding of at least 25% in the share capital of the other company for an uninterrupted period of at least one year. This holding condition will also be fulfilled if a third company established within the EU holds or has had a direct or indirect holding of at least 25% in the share capital of both associated companies for an uninterrupted period of at least one year;
   - the rights, debt receivables or loans on which interest is paid may not be part of the assets of an establishment held by the recipient of the interest outside the EU.

[262] Non-resident entities that do not qualify for the aforementioned exemptions may benefit from a reduced withholding tax rate or a withholding tax exemption under one of Belgium's bilateral tax treaties. Subject to conditions, treaties may provide for a 10%, 5% or even nil rate (e.g., Article 11 of the new tax treaty between Belgium and the USA).

Capital Gains Taxation: Corporate Entities

[263] The income tax treatment of capital gains depends on the kind of assets realized and the person receiving the capital gains. In principle, capital gains realized by companies subject to Belgian corporation tax or non-resident corporation tax are deemed to be taxable business profits, and are taxed at the applicable corporation tax rate. Capital losses realized on assets other than shares are in principle tax deductible.

[264] Capital gains realized on tangible or intangible fixed assets invested in the company for at least five years may benefit from a tax deferral. This will require, *inter alia*, reinvestment of the free amount of the proceeds received in fiscally depreciable tangible or intangible fixed assets that will be used for the business of the company in the European Economic Area. It will also require fulfilment of an intangibility condition for the amount of the realized capital gain (sections 47 and 190, second paragraph, ITC92). In this case, the capital gains will be taxed proportionally, in accordance with any depreciation applied to the assets acquired with the proceeds of the sale.

[265] Capital gains realized by Belgian-resident companies on the sale of shares are in principle subject to the full corporate tax rate. A reduced rate of 25.75% (i.e., 25% plus a 3% crisis surcharge calculated on the 25%) may apply provided that the company in which the participation was held, meets the 'taxation condition' of the DRD regime. If this condition is met and the Belgian-resident vendor has held the shares in full ownership for at least one year, the realized capital gain will be exempt, provided that the vendor qualifies as a small company in the sense of section 15 of the Companies Code. If the latter condition is not met, the capital gain will be subject to a separate tax of 0.412% tax (incl. the 3% crisis surcharge). For the application of this 0.412% tax, the amount of the qualifying capital gain may not be reduced by means of tax losses, the DRD or the notional interest deduction. In general, capital losses realized on shares are not deductible for corporation tax purposes, except where the issuer of the shares is being liquidated. In that case, an amount equal to the loss of fiscally paid-up capital represented by the transferred shares will be tax deductible (section 198(1), seventh paragraph, ITC92).

[266] Non-resident companies that have not invested their shares in a Belgian permanent establishment will normally be treaty-protected from Belgian capital gains taxation. The power to tax the capital gains realized by such companies will normally inure to the company's State of tax residence. However, if the shares were invested in a Belgian permanent establishment, the non-resident shareholder will be subject to the same capital gains tax regime as Belgian-resident companies.

[267] In addition, capital gains realized in connection with a merger, a division or a transaction equated to a merger by acquisition or to a division may qualify for a full corporation tax exemption in the hands of a Belgian-resident company involved in such a transaction. Any capital contribution made pursuant to such a transaction should be remunerated with newly issued shares. The corporation tax exemption is subject to the following conditions (section 211, first paragraph, ITC92):

- (i) the absorbing company or the company benefiting from the transaction must qualify as a Belgian-resident company or as an intra-European company ('IEC');
- (ii) the transaction must be carried out in accordance with the Companies Code and, if relevant, the similar company law rules of applicable to IECs; and
- (iii) the transaction must fulfil the so-called 'valid commercial reasons' test, i.e., it must not have tax evasion or tax avoidance as its main purpose or one of its main purposes.

[268] If these conditions are fulfilled but the consideration does not entirely comprise newly issued shares, then the tax-exempt reserves will be taxable in proportion to the amount of the distribution that is not compensated in shares, unless these reserves are re-invested. However, any recorded but unrealized capital gains, capital gains qualifying for a tax deferral, capital grants or capital gains realized in connection with the transaction will in any event remain free from corporation tax (section 211, second paragraph, ITC92). Conditions will, however, apply if the restructuring has a cross-border character.

[269] Where the above conditions are not fulfilled, the transaction in question will be deemed a liquidation of the company for corporation tax purposes. In that case, the positive difference between the deemed distributions in cash, securities or any other form, and the carrying value of the paid-up capital will be considered a distributed dividend. This will trigger taxation of latent capital gains and all tax-exempt reserves, and will also trigger a 27% withholding tax on all reserves distributed in excess of the fiscally paid-in capital.

Capital Gains Taxation: Individuals

[270] The income tax treatment of capital gains realized by individuals also depends on the kind of assets realized.

[271] Capital gains realized on the transfer of a major holding within the framework of the normal management of private assets are treated as miscellaneous income. They are taxed separately at a rate of 16.5% (plus municipal surcharges) according to the following circumstances and conditions:

(i) the shares must be provided by a Belgian company;
(ii) the transfer must be made to a non-resident legal entity having its tax residence outside the European Economic Area;
(iii) the transfer must be made in return for payment; and
(iv) the transferred shares must be part of a major holding in the issuing company, i.e., the grantor must throughout the previous five years, alone or together with a member of his group, directly or indirectly have held more than 25% of the shares in the issuing company.

[272] However, there is a full exemption for capital gains realized within the framework of normal transactions of private asset management following transfer of a major holding to:

(i) a Belgian-resident individual subject to Belgian personal income tax;
(ii) a Belgian non-resident individual subject to non-resident personal income tax;
(iii) a Belgian-resident company subject to corporation tax;
(iv) a Belgian-resident legal entity subject to Belgian tax on legal entities;
(v) a foreign association without legal personality that is not constituted under a legal form similar to a Belgian company and, therefore, is not subject to corporate non-resident taxes.

[273] The aforementioned exemption suffers an important exception under the form of the so-called speculation tax. As of 1 January 2016, capital gains realized in relation to shares in listed companies, options, warrants and certificate shares held for a period of less than six months, are taxable at a rate of 33%. This taxation applies even if the sale qualifies as a normal act of asset management.

Mergers and Acquisitions

Choice of the Method of Acquisition

[274] The choice of acquisition method and, in particular, the choice between a transfer of assets or a transfer of shares largely depends on tax considerations dictated by the composition of the assets, how long they have been held and the capacity in which they have been held. Hence, there can be no general rule, and each case must be examined on the basis of its own merits.

[275] In general, however, if the seller is an individual, in principle he will not be subject to income tax on any capital gains he might realize on a sale of shares, except in cases where the so-called speculation tax may apply. The seller will therefore derive little benefit from a transfer of assets. He would then have to wind up the company, in which case all latent capital gains and tax-exempt reserves would become taxable, and any liquidation surplus received would be subject to withholding tax. In addition, since there is no going concern upon a transfer of assets, any carryover losses within the transferor cannot be reclaimed by the transferee.

Tax Considerations Relating to the Purchaser

[276] From the purchaser's point of view, an acquisition of assets may be preferred to a sale of shares owing to the characteristics of the assets. If the purchaser acquires assets, he will benefit from a 'step-up' in value, enabling tax-deductible depreciation and write-downs starting from the assets' market value. If the purchaser has entered into a loan agreement in order to fund acquisition of the assets, the interest cost will in principle be fully tax deductible.

[277] A transfer of shares, on the other hand, provides the purchaser with non-depreciable assets. Moreover, any impairment of the acquired shares will not be tax deductible, save for the exception for losses of paid-up capital where the company issuing the shares is liquidated. If the purchaser has entered into a loan agreement in order to fund the share acquisition, then dividends may be distributed to ensure repayment of the loan. The full interest cost will be tax deductible. However, the dividends distributed in order to pay the interest burden will only be 95% deductible under the DRD regime. This disadvantage is less significant where the purchaser's profits derive from sources other than dividends distributed by the newly acquired company, for example profits from a separate business. A merger between the purchasing company and the offeree company might also be considered under the tax-exempt regime described below.

Neutrality of Mergers and Divisions

[278] Under Belgian tax law, mergers, divisions and equivalent transactions are treated favourably, and may benefit from a corporation tax exemption. Following implementation of the EU Merger Directive of 23 July 1990 (90/434/EC), as codified by the Directive of 19 October 2009 (2009/133/EC), ('the Directive') into Belgian domestic legislation also intra-European reorganizations may benefit – to a certain extent – from tax neutrality (sections 211 et seq., ITC92).

[279] The exemption regime or 'neutrality regime' is subject to the following conditions:

(i) The absorbing company or the company benefiting from the transaction must qualify as a Belgian-resident company, or as an 'IEC', i.e., a company that has a legal form listed in the annex to the Directive, has its tax residence outside Belgium in another EU Member State and is subject to a normal corporation tax regime.
(ii) The transaction must be carried out in accordance with the Companies Code and, if relevant, the similar company law rules applicable to IECs.
(iii) The transaction must meet the so-called 'valid commercial reasons' test, i.e., not have tax evasion or tax avoidance as its main purpose or as one of its main purposes.

[280] Following a decision by the Court of Cassation in December 2007 and a subsequent amendment of the ITC92, this test, which is almost identical to that in the Directive, should be met in order to qualify as a fully exempted merger or division. If the transaction is not based on valid commercial reasons, such as restructuring or rationalization of the activities of the companies involved, then there may be a presumption that its main purpose or one of its main purposes is tax evasion or tax avoidance, unless the taxpayer can prove the contrary.

[281] If the neutrality regime applies, all capital gains realized at the level of the offeree company and arising from the merger are tax-exempt. Any capital gains on asset revaluation or other capital gains that are subject to a system of tax deferral, are transferred without tax liability to the absorbing company. From an accounting point of view, the absorbing company must value the transferred assets as appearing in the books of the offeree company prior to the transaction. This valuation rule is similar from a corporation tax point of view. Therefore, depreciation, investment deductions, capital grants, capital gains or losses on the transferred assets, and the capital to be taken into account within the absorbing or receiving company, are determined as if the transaction had not taken place. This rule is equally applicable to tax-exempted reserves as well as provisions, receivables, etc.

[282] If the transaction does not qualify for the neutrality regime, it will be treated as a liquidation of the company. Consequently, any 'hidden' reserves or capital gains (plus-values latentes/latente meerwaarden) that were treated as tax-exempt reserves or that only arise pursuant to the transaction, will be deemed realized and will be taxable at the applicable corporation tax rate. The acquiring company will benefit from a step-up in value of the acquired assets, meaning that the depreciable value of the assets is higher. It may therefore be that in some cases, the application of the liquidation regimet to the transaction would be more advantageous, especially if the offeree company and/or the absorbing company have a substantial sum of carryover losses. Under the liquidation regime, no limits apply to the deduction of carryover losses. The reduction rule described below does not apply.

[283] The deduction of carryover losses is treated differently depending on whether the merger, division or equivalent transaction is tax-exempt under section 211 of the ITC92 or is deemed equivalent to a liquidation of the company and taxed accordingly.

[284] If a taxed transaction is selected, i.e., one of the three conditions above is not fulfilled, then there will be no transfer of carryover losses. However, if the transaction is performed under the neutrality regime, by contrast with the rule that tax losses can only be used by the company that incurred them, the tax losses of the absorbed company can shift to the surviving company. Within certain limits, the pre-merger losses of the surviving company continue to be deductible according to the following fraction:

$$\frac{\text{Fiscal net value of the absorbing company, pre-merger}}{\text{Fiscal net value of the absorbing company + Fiscal net value of the assets of the absorbed company, \textbf{both} pre-merger}}$$

The pre-merger losses of the absorbed company also continue to be deductible at the level of the surviving company according to the following fraction:

$$\frac{\text{Fiscal net value of the absorbed company, pre-merger}}{\text{Fiscal net value of the absorbing company + Fiscal net value of the assets of the absorbed company, \textbf{both} pre-merger}}$$

[285] The following example of a merger by absorption illustrates how these formulae work in practice:

Target/Absorbed Company	*Absorbing Company*
Net fiscal value of assets: 1 000	Net fiscal value of assets: 2 000
Losses carried forward: 300	Losses carried forward: 900

[286] The losses of the absorbed company (300) are transferred proportionally at a rate of 1 000 (net fiscal value of the absorbed company) over 3 000 (aggregate net fiscal value of both the absorbed company and the absorbing company), i.e., 300 x 1/3 = 100.

[287] The losses of the absorbing company (900) are transferred proportionally at a rate of 2 000 (net fiscal value of the absorbing company) over 3 000, i.e., 900 x 2/3 = 600.

[288] As a consequence, the absorbed company's losses and the absorbing company's carryover losses will continue to be deductible at the level of the newly merged company in an amount of 700 (100 + 600).

Parent-Subsidiary Merger

[289] Where a parent company takes over one of its subsidiaries, the shares owned by the absorbing company in the offeree company are cancelled and the equity of the offeree company is reduced proportionally (section 703, second paragraph, Companies Code and section 78, sixth paragraph, Royal Decree implementing the Companies Code). From a corporation tax point of view, this equity reduction may trigger corporation tax on the tax-exempt reserves thereby affected, unless the parent company takes over the exempt reserves from its subsidiary. The takeover can be realized via the creation of a reserve account combined with creation of a negative taxed reserve incorporated in capital.

[290] At the level of the parent company, the dividend deemed distributed upon cancellation of its shareholding in the offeree company may benefit from 100% DRD, even if the DRD's holding condition requirements are not met.

Merger of a Belgian Company into an Intra-European Company ('IEC')

[291] When a Belgian company merges into an IEC, the tax-neutrality regime is subject to additional conditions whose aim is to avoid the disappearance of taxable assets in Belgium further to the merger:

(a) components of the Belgian company must be taken over and used by a Belgian establishment (i.e., the Belgian domestic equivalent of a permanent establishment) of the IEC (pre-existing or resulting from the merger) and must contribute to the results that form part of the tax base of the Belgian establishment;
(b) the tax-exempt reserves of the Belgian company must show up in the own funds of the Belgian establishment.

[292] For this purpose, Belgian corporation tax law has created the concept of own funds for Belgian establishments, which are the sum of (1) their exempt reserves; (2) their taxed reserves; and (3) the capital contribution at the Belgian establishment's disposal.

[293] The transfer of the assets will be tax-neutral such that the tax characteristics of these components will be maintained within the Belgian establishment.

[294] The treatment of the transfer of carryover losses to the Belgian establishment differs according to whether or not the IEC already has an existing Belgian establishment prior to the merger. If the absorbing company does not have such an establishment prior to the merger, losses carried forward will be 100% transferred and deductible at the level of the Belgian establishment. Otherwise, the following limitations will be applicable.

[295] Pre-merger losses of the Belgian target continue to be deductible at the level of the Belgian establishment according to the following fraction:

$$\frac{\text{Fiscal net value of the transferred assets, pre-merger}}{\text{Fiscal net value of the Belgian establishment} + \text{Fiscal net value of the transferred assets, both pre-merger}}$$

[273] And pre-merger losses of the Belgian establishment continue to be deductible according to the following fraction:

$$\frac{\text{Fiscal net value of the Belgian establishment, pre-merger}}{\text{Fiscal net value of the Belgian establishment} + \text{Fiscal net value of the transferred assets, both pre-merger}}$$

Merger of an IEC into a Belgian Company

[296] As a consequence of the tax-neutral regime in the case of the merger of an IEC without a Belgian establishment into a Belgian company, the Belgian company keeps the components of the IEC in a foreign permanent establishment, the profits of which will normally be exempt in Belgium.

[297] According to the corporation tax rules, subsequent capital gains or losses, depreciation and reductions or increases in value realized on components situated abroad but received by a resident company are calculated by reference to the book value at the time of the merger. An exception to this rule applies for capital losses, depreciations and value reductions realized on assets when the book value of said assets was re-evaluated prior to the merger without being effectively taxed in the State where the IEC is established.

[298] According to Belgian standards, the fiscal capital of the Belgian company will be increased by the paid-up capital of the IEC and the rest of the IEC's own funds will be treated as taxed reserves, save for pre-merger exempt reserves connected to any Belgian establishment of the IEC.

[299] Previous tax losses of the Belgian company continue to be 100% deductible where IEC has no Belgian establishment pre-merger.

Merger of an IEC with a Belgian Establishment into Another IEC or into a Belgian Company

[300] The tax-neutrality regime will only apply in the case of a merger of an IEC with Belgian establishment into another IEC or into a Belgian company if the following conditions are fulfilled:

(i) the merger must be realized under the tax-neutrality regime of the Member State of the absorbed IEC;
(ii) the merger must be realized in conformity with the Companies Code and similar company law rules applicable to the absorbed IEC;
(iii) the anti-abuse provision mentioned above must be adhered to;
(iv) components of the IEC must be used or preserved within the Belgian establishment and must contribute to the results of the establishment.

[301] As a consequence of the tax-neutrality regime, recorded but untaxed gains, untaxed capital subsidies and contribution gains are exempt. Moreover, there will be no other taxation provided the contribution is remunerated by shares or provided the exempt reserves of the absorbed IEC are taken over by the Belgian company or by the absorbing IEC in a Belgian establishment.

[302] Tax losses incurred in the Belgian establishment will transfer or be deductible according to the following fraction:

$$\frac{\text{Fiscal Net value Belgian establishment, pre-merger}}{\text{Fiscal Net Value of the absorbing company} + \text{Fiscal Net Value Belgian establishment, both pre-merger}}$$

Cross-Border Contribution of a Line of Business/Assets by Universal Transfer

[303] Belgian tax law has also set up a tax-exemption regime applicable to the cross-border contribution of a line of business (branche d'activité/bedrijfstak) as a part of a going concern, or a universal transfer of assets (universalité de biens/algemeenheid van goederen) to an IEC in return for shares. The exemption rules for corporation tax purposes apply if the following conditions are met:

(i) the capital contribution must be remunerated with shares representing the share capital of the company benefiting from the transaction;
(ii) the contribution to the IEC must be made in accordance with the Companies Code and similar rules applicable to the IEC;
(iii) the contribution must meet the 'valid commercial reasons' test;
(iv) the contributed components must be maintained and used by the IEC in a Belgian establishment and must contribute to its results.

[304] If these conditions are fulfilled, capital gains realized on the assets transferred will be temporarily exempt from taxation. If these capital gains have to be expressed for accounting purposes at the level of the company benefiting from the transaction, then the corporation tax exemption will be subject to a condition of intangibility (section 190, third paragraph, ITC92).

[305] The absorbing company must value the transferred assets and liabilities at their net tax value as appearing in the books of the transferring company before the transfer, and the transferor company must book the shares received at that same value.

[306] Under certain conditions a tax-exemption regime also applies to the cross-border contribution of a line of business as part of a going-concern business, or of assets by way of a universal transfer of an IEC to a Belgian-resident company.

VAT and Registration Duties

[307] For Belgian VAT purposes, any universal transfer of assets or of a line of business by way of a capital contribution or in any other way is not considered a vatable supply of goods or services, irrespective of whether the transaction is made for value or free of charge. This requires the party benefiting from the transaction to qualify as a vatpayer that would be able to deduct input VAT were it is chargeable on the transfer (section 11, VAT Code). If indeed the transfer does not qualify as a vatable transaction, then the party benefiting from the transaction will continue in the shoes of the transferring company for VAT purposes. Moreover, these transactions will also not qualify as a vatable supply of services (section 18, third paragraph, VAT Code).

[308] Following the transaction and in terms of sections 11 and 18, third paragraph, of the VAT Code, the party benefiting from the transaction will assume the VAT obligations formerly arising at the level of the transferring company: it will have to file a VAT return each month or quarter as the case may be, be subject to revision of the VAT incurred on the goods it has acquired, etc.

[309] If the above 'VAT neutrality' conditions do not apply, the transfer of goods will be subject to the normal VAT regime, possibly triggering input VAT. The deduction of input VAT incurred on the transaction by the company benefiting from the transaction will in this case only depend on its own VAT status.

[310] For the purposes of registration duties, an exemption from capital duty has been introduced into Belgian domestic law under the aforementioned EU Merger Directive (section 117, Registration Duties Code). Hence, under certain conditions, a universal transfer of assets or a transfer of a line of business will qualify for an exemption from registration duties. Moreover, the exemption can equally apply to an exchange of shares. If the transaction does not qualify under these latter conditions, then the normal capital duty will apply. However, as from 1 January 2006, the capital duty rate was reduced to nil. Therefore, no *ad valorem* registration duties will be chargeable on capital contributions made by resident or non-resident corporate entities in Belgium except in the case of a so-called 'mixed contribution', i.e., a contribution that is not entirely remunerated by shares, in which case the ordinary registration duty on transfers of real property may apply.

[311] However, a transfer of shares undertaken via a bank or stockbroker will trigger stock exchange tax. The usual tax rate is 0.17% on each sale and purchase, up to a maximum of EUR500 per transaction and per party. As for a purchase of shares, the taxable basis will comprise all payments due by the purchaser, not including the broker's fees. For a sale of shares, the taxable basis will be the payment receivable by the seller, again excluding the broker's fees.

EMPLOYMENT CONSIDERATIONS

Information to be Given to the Workforce

[312] An employer is under an obligation to inform the workers' representatives, i.e., the works council, failing which the trade union delegation, failing which the committee for prevention and protection at work, (a) any time events occur that are liable to entail serious consequences for the undertaking; and (b) in all cases where internal decisions are taken that are likely to have major repercussions within the undertaking.

[313] In the case of a merger, concentration, division, transfer, closure, collective dismissal or other major change to the structure of an undertaking, the workers' representatives of the (the works council, failing which the trade union delegation, failing which the committee for prevention and protection at work must be informed and consulted before any formal decision is taken and in any event before the change is made public.

[314] In particular, the workers' representatives must be consulted and must have the opportunity to give their views on all issues having major repercussions on the employment prospects of the workforce, the organization of the work and employment policy in general, and with regard to the means to be deployed to avoid dismissals and transfers. It must be underlined that the consultation must take place before the event: in order to avoid presenting the workers' representatives with a fait accompli, they must be consulted prior to the decision that it falls to the employer to take (e.g., before the closing of the intended transaction).

[315] In practice, this procedure is carried out in several phases:

(a) First, the employer informs the workers' representatives. This intimation is accompanied by comments by the employer as to the anticipated consequences of the decision to be taken on further development of the undertaking's business and the workers' situation.
(b) Then comes consultation. The essence is that there should be an exchange of views between the employer's representatives, on the one hand, and the workers' representatives, on the other. The latter must have the opportunity to ask questions and make any criticisms, suggestions and objections, whether their opinions are unanimous or divergent.
(c) Finally, in order to ensure continuity of the dialogue, the employer should indicate either immediately or during the next meeting what heed the employer intends to pay or has given to the opinions, suggestions or objections formulated by the workers' representatives.
(d) For evidence purposes, to end the information and consultation procedure with the workers' representatives, it is advisable to have them sign a document in which they recognize that the employer duly complied with its information and consultation obligations towards them. The signature of such document is however not required by law.

[316] Consultation of the workers' representatives in no way affects the decision-making prerogative that ultimately falls to the employer. Furthermore, the workers' representatives are subject to a duty of discretion and confidentiality concerning the information that is passed to them by the employer and concerning the topics discussed during the consultation process. Criminal penalties are laid down, although in practice it is extremely difficult to gather sufficient evidence of an infringement to justify civil penalties (e.g., dismissal for serious misconduct) or a prosecution. In order to ensure confidentiality, the employer may state explicitly that the information and the topics discussed during the consultation process are confidential and that, if they are divulged in advance, this could damage the business.

[317] Criminal penalties are laid down if the employer does not adhere to the information and consultation obligation (with a fine of up to EUR3 000 per worker, up to a maximum of EUR300 000. Additional penalties apply in cases of infringement of the collective dismissal and/or closure of undertakings procedure (*see* below). Moreover, the workers or the trade union may also lodge summary proceedings to compel the employer to comply with its information and consultation duties.

[318] Where there is no works council or trade union delegation, the employer must comply with the information obligations mentioned above and initiate consultation with the members of the committee for prevention and protection at work. Should there be no worker representative body in the enterprise, case law indicates that it is best practice to provide each of the workers with information similar to that referred to above.

[319] Under Community Directive 94/95 of the Council of the European Union dated 22 September 1994 concerning the institution of European works councils, which has been transposed into Belgian law, in all cases where the measure contemplated considerably affects the workers' interests (e.g., moving to new premises, closure of a part of the business, collective dismissals), information has to be provided to, and there has to be consultation with, the European works council, if there is one. Collective bargaining agreement (CBA) no. 84 of 6 October 2004 stipulates specific provisions dealing with the information and consultation of staff working in a European company (*societas europaea*, SE).

Termination of Employment Contracts

[320] This section briefly discusses certain aspects of Belgian law that are relevant to an employer when considering the termination of employment contracts in Belgium. Although the legal status of blue-collar and white-collar workers was partially harmonized by a legal reform which became effective in 2014, it is still important to distinguish between blue-collar workers, who essentially perform work of a manual nature, and white-collar workers, who essentially carry out work of an intellectual nature.

[321] Different rules may apply to white-collar workers and to blue-collar workers in case of termination of the employment contract or in connection with restructuring processes such as collective dismissal or closure of undertaking).

Notice Period or Compensation in Lieu of Notice

General Principles

[322] Under Belgian law, every person employed for an undefined period of time and who is dismissed for reasons other than serious cause (*motif grave / dringende reden*), is entitled to a period of notice in advance of the date of dismissal or, if the worker does not work out the notice period, to the payment of an indemnity in lieu of the notice. Consequently, the employer must either:

- Give the worker prior notice in advance of the termination, during which time the worker continues to work.
- Pay an indemnity in lieu of notice in the event of immediate termination of the contract. The indemnity in lieu of notice is equivalent to the remuneration that the worker would have earned during the notice period, if such a notice period had been performed (*see* below).

[323] It results from the foregoing that, in case of unilateral termination of an employment contract, the first step is to determine the length of the notice period which must be given to the worker.

[324] If, in the case of a dismissal, the worker is asked to work out the notice period, formal conditions relating to timing and form have to be complied with by the employer when sending the notice, failing which the notice will be deemed to be void and the employment contract will be deemed to be wrongfully terminated with immediate effect, resulting in an obligation to pay compensation in lieu of notice (the notice must be sent by registered mail or by bailiff notification, must mention the date of commencement of the notice period, the length of the notice period, and must be written in either Dutch, French or German depending on certain circumstances set forth by law. These formal requirements are not mandatory in case of dismissal with immediate effect and payment of an indemnity in lieu of notice.

[325] The rules applicable in case of termination of employment contracts have fundamentally changed since the entry into force of new legislation on 1 January 2014.

[326] Generally speaking, it may be said that the rules applicable in case of termination of employment contracts are now similar for blue-collar workers and white-collar workers, which was not the case prior to 1 January 2014. As from 1 January 2014, the length of the notice period to be given in case of dismissal is expressed in a certain number of weeks, set on the basis of the seniority level acquired by the worker at the time of the dismissal.

[327] However, the rules for determining the length of the applicable notice period vary depending on the level of seniority acquired prior to 31 December 2013 and after 1 January 2014.

[328] The length of the notice period relating to seniority acquired prior to 31 December 2013 is in principle calculated in accordance with the termination rules as they were applicable on 31 December 2013.

[329] Consequently, in respect of seniority acquired prior to 31 December 2013, the rules for calculating the notice period to which a worker is entitled are not entirely harmonized between blue-collar and white-collar workers, as prior to that date, the calculation of the notice period was different for blue-collar workers and for white-collar workers.

[330] The total notice period to which a worker is entitled in case of dismissal is in principle equal to the sum of: (i) the notice period relating to the seniority acquired prior to 31 December 2013; and (ii) the notice period relating to seniority acquired after 1 January 2014.

[331] In case of unilateral termination of employment contracts concluded for an indefinite duration, the rules applicable for calculating the notice periods to be given by the employer to the workers in respect of seniority acquired after 1 January 2014, are the same for blue-collar and white-collar workers and may be summarized as follows (keeping in mind that special rules apply to specific worker categories, defined by law):

seniority	*notice period (weeks)*	*seniority*	*notice period (weeks)*
0-3 months	2	9-10 years	30
3-6 months	4	10-11 years	33
6-9 months	6	11-12 years	36
9-12 months	7	12-13 years	39
12-15 months	8	13-14 years	42
15-18 months	9	14-15 years	45
18-21 months	10	15-16 years	48
21-24 months	11	16-17 years	51
2-3 years	12	17-18 years	54
3-4 years	13	18-19 years	57
4 - 5 years	15	19 - 20 years	60
5 - 6 years	18	20 - 21 years	62
6 - 7 years	21	21- 22 years	63
7 - 8 years	24	22 - 23 years	64
8 - 9 years	27	+ 1 year	+ 1

Specific Provisions for White-Collar Workers

[332] For workers considered as white-collar workers as at 31 December 2013, the notice period for seniority acquired prior to 31 December 2013 is calculated as follows:

- Workers with an annual base remuneration of less than EUR32 254 as at 31 December 2013 are entitled to a notice period of three months for each five year period of service or part thereof.
- Workers with an annual base remuneration of EUR32 254 or more as at 31 December 2013 are entitled to a notice period of one month for each year of service or part thereof.

Specific Provisions for Blue-Collar Workers

[333] For workers considered as blue-collar workers as at 31 December 2013, the notice period relating to seniority acquired prior to 31 December 2013 is in principle calculated in accordance with the rules applicable in the relevant industry sector prior to that date. In most industry sectors, these rules are set forth in CBAs or in Royal Decree.

The Indemnity in Lieu of Notice

[334] The indemnity in lieu of notice corresponds to the remuneration that the worker would have received during the notice period, had the worker continued working during said notice period.

[335] The remuneration must include, in addition to the basic remuneration, all other advantages and fringe benefits to which the worker is entitled within the framework of his employment contract, e.g., year-end bonus, employer contributions to a group or health insurance plan, meal vouchers, incentive bonuses, merit bonuses, etc.

Protected Workers

[336] Very specific legal provisions are also applicable to members of, and candidates for, a company's works council or committee for prevention and protection at work, as is the case for union representatives and other 'protected workers', e.g., time credit leave, pregnant workers, workers on parental leave, etc. If these workers are dismissed, they are generally entitled to significant compensation, save when the specific procedure has been complied with or when the employer can establish that the dismissal is not based on a proscribed reason.

Closure of an Undertaking

[337] In addition to the rules described above relating to the calculation of notice periods, the Act of 26 June 2002 governs the basic principles to be respected in case of closure of an undertaking. 'Undertaking' means a technical operating unit as defined under the 1948 Act on the organization of the economy. This means that this legislation does not necessarily apply to the legal entity as such, but to each division of the company, or a combination of companies, that has a degree of autonomy and independence on the basis of economic and corporate criteria. Several legal entities can also form one single technical operating unit. The act seeks among others to require employers to furnish certain information to enable such workers to find new jobs, and to make the employer pay a specific closure indemnity for the loss suffered by the workers as a result of closure of the undertaking.

Scope

[338] Pursuant to the Act of 26 June 2002, a closure is deemed to have taken place where the following cumulative conditions are met: (a) the principal activity of the undertaking or one of its divisions definitively ceases; (b) the number of workers whose employment is terminated exceeds 75% of the average number of persons employed in the undertaking or the relevant part thereof for the calendar year preceding cessation of the principal activity and (c) the undertaking or division employs at least twenty workers on average during the four quarters preceding the quarter in which the main activity has been definitively terminated.

[339] In nearly all cases, a closure of an undertaking or closure of a division thereof will also be considered as a collective dismissal (*see* below). This means that both the legislation on closure of undertakings and the legislation on collective dismissals should be complied with.

Duty of Information

[340] The procedure laid down in the Royal Decree of 23 March 2007 must be followed:

(a) there is a duty to provide information beforehand to the workers, the workers' representatives (works council, failing which the trade union delegation, failing which the committee for prevention and protection at work), the workers themselves and certain public authorities (various government departments). The information given must include certain compulsory particulars (a.o. name and address of the undertaking, nature of the undertaking's business, anticipated date of closure, staff list);
(b) at the latest on the 15th day after termination of the employment contracts, the employer must provide certain information to the Closure Fund.

Closure Indemnity

[341] A closure indemnity is due:

(a) only to workers who are employed under an employment contract for an undefined period;
(ii) to workers having been in continuous employment for at least one year;
(iii) to workers who are dismissed for reasons other than serious misconduct, during the period from 18 (for white-collar workers) or twelve months (for blue-collar workers) before the date of closure to twelve months after that date; and
(iv) to workers who were not offered a new job at the same level of remuneration and seniority as in their previous jobs and to workers who have been offered such a new job but have been dismissed by their new employers within six months;
(v) to workers who did not reach the legal retirement age or cannot benefit from the system of unemployment with company allowances (formerly known as bridge pension);
(vi) to workers who do not benefit from a transitional benefit in the sense of the Act of 26 June 2002.

Amount of the Closure Indemnity

[342] The closure indemnity is composed of the following elements:

- EUR156.88 per year of seniority in the undertaking, with a maximum of twenty times this amount (this amount was set as at 1 June 2016 and is regularly subject to indexation).

- For workers aged over 45, additional compensation of EUR156.88 for each year over 45, with a maximum of nineteen times this amount (this amount was again set as at 1 June 2016 and is regularly subject to indexation); each year's seniority is construed as each year's seniority within the undertaking from age 45.
- A closure indemnity is exempt from social security contributions provided that it does not exceed the aforementioned maximum limits.

[343] Compensation for closure of an undertaking cannot be paid in addition to the collective dismissal indemnity, which could be due in the framework of a collective dismissal as discussed below.

Collective Dismissals

Preamble

[344] 'Collective dismissal' means the dismissal of a group of workers over the course of a certain period. The legal definition of a collective dismissal varies depending on the topic at stake (information and consultation requirements, entitlement to the collective dismissal indemnity, etc.). In the event of a collective dismissal, in addition to the rules that apply to all cases of dismissal, the following additional requirements could apply:

- a specific preliminary information and consultation procedure should be complied with, to be started as soon as the employer has the intention to proceed to a collective dismissal (so before taking the actual decision to proceed thereto), during which certain information has to be provided;
- the creation of an employment action group (*cellule pour l'emploi / tewerkstellingscel*) at the end of the information and consultation procedure;
- the entering into a social plan, providing for the terms and conditions of termination of the employment contract of the workers concerned by the collective dismissal; and
- the worker could be entitled to a specific collective dismissal indemnity.

Information and Consultation Procedures

[345] For the purposes of the regulations relating to the obligation to notify, 'collective dismissal' means any dismissal for one or more reasons that have nothing to do with the inherent qualities of the worker him or herself, and that affect a certain number of workers:

(i) numbering at least ten in companies that had an average workforce of more than 20 and less than 100 workers over the calendar year preceding the dismissal;
(ii) representing at least 10% of the number of workers in companies that had an average workforce of 100 or more and less than 300 workers during the calendar year preceding the dismissal;

(iii) numbering at least 30 in companies that had an average workforce of 300 or more workers during the calendar year preceding the dismissal.

[346] To trigger the information and consultation procedure, applicable in case of collective dismissals, the dismissals must be effected (i.e., either notified or the employment contract effectively terminated):

(i) either over an uninterrupted period of sixty days; or
(ii) if the collective dismissal procedure is not combined with a closure of undertakings procedure, within a period of sixty days following the first sixty day period referred to above; or
(iii) if the collective dismissal procedure is combined with a closure of undertakings procedure within the period beginning at the end of the initial period of sixty days referred to above and that ends with the closure of the undertaking.

Consultation with Workers' Representatives

[347] As soon as the employer envisages implementing a collective dismissal, it must advise the workers' representatives thereof and enter into consultation with them. This notification and consultation is carried out within the works council or, failing this, with the trade union delegation or, failing this, with the committee for prevention and protection at work, or, failing this, with the staff themselves. In the absence of any worker representative bodies it is nevertheless common that the workers appoint representatives, especially in relation to negotiation of a social plan, as defined below, if any.

[348] The consultations involve the possibilities of avoiding or reducing the collective dismissal as well as mitigating the consequences. In this regard, the employer must provide the workers' representatives with all obligatory information.

[349] The most important point in this regard is that the information and consultation should take place *before any decision is made,* i.e., when the employer is only contemplating whether or not to proceed with a collective dismissal.

Notifying the Collective Dismissal to the Regional Employment Office

[350] The employer must notify the collective dismissal to the director of the subregional employment office in the area where the company is situated (FOREM, Actiris, or VDAB). The notification must contain certain mandatory information. The employer may not serve notice on the workers concerned until expiry of a waiting period of thirty days starting with the day on which notice is given. In certain cases, the period will be reduced, or extended to a maximum of sixty days.

Negotiation of a Social Plan

[351] A social plan should in this respect be understood as an overall agreement with the workers and their representatives on the procedures for the restructuring (compensation to be paid, etc.) and, if relevant, the arrangements that have been made for the workers that are not dismissed (e.g., a commitment by the employer not to lay staff off for one or two years). A redundancy scheme generally lists the statutory rights of the workers, and includes provisions that are the result of collective bargaining (e.g., compensation in lieu of notice exceeding the workers' statutory entitlements).

[352] Although the employer has no legal duty to enter into a social plan, it may have a clear interest in offering the workers more than their minimum entitlements in order to achieve an agreement with the workers and their representatives:

(a) The worker representatives could challenge compliance with the collective dismissal procedure by formulating objections in this regard. The existence of objections by the worker representatives on the collective dismissal procedure leaves room for claims by the individual workers(*see* below).

(b) If the employer refuses to negotiate a social plan, it is almost certain that the joint committee will refuse authorization to dismiss any (elected or unelected) candidates in the so-called 'social elections' for economic or technical reasons. The joint committee can only authorize the dismissals if all the members unanimously decide in favour, and trade union representatives on the joint committee need not give reasons for refusing.

(c) Under given circumstances, the entering into a social plan is required by law and in particular (i) in order for the employer to be recognized as a 'company in difficulties' or a 'company in restructuring' by the employment authorities, whereby the minimum age to take up the regime of unemployment with company allowances (UCA, formerly known as bridge pension), could under given circumstances be reduced to 56 year of age (57 year of age as from 1 January 2017), instead of the general age limit of 62 years, and whereby the employer could benefit from reduced social security contributions on the UCA-allowances and (ii) obtaining a 'restructuring card' for the employees, whereby some payments could be reclaimed from the authorities by the employer.

(d) Moreover, negotiation of a social plan is widespread practice in Belgium, such that, in the event of a restructuring of a Belgian company, the workers and their trade unions will expect the employer to be willing to negotiate a social plan, under which additional benefits are provided for. In the overwhelming majority of restructuring situations, this is in effect the case, although some social plans merely list the legal entitlements of the workers and include a very limited number of 'voluntary' commitments by the employer.

(e) Finally, the majority of employers do in fact negotiate a social plan, and if an employer refused to do so, there is a very considerable risk that the trade unions would organize industrial action.

Penalties

[353] In the event the employer does not properly inform and consult with the worker representative bodies, a multitude of sanctions can be imposed:

- The most draconian sanction is that stipulated in the so-called Renault Act. Under this act, workers dismissed during the collective dismissal procedure can initiate individual action if the information and consultation procedure is not complied with. The workers can no longer initiate any action if the workers' representatives have not objected to noncompliance with the procedure during the period of thirty days following intimation of the second notification to the director.
- If employment court upheld a claim by an worker, the employer basically could not terminate the employment contract at any time until the collective dismissal procedure had been properly gone through.
- If the workers concerned have not yet been dismissed, the employment court may, in summary proceedings, order suspension of the ongoing collective dismissal procedure and even recommencement of the procedure.
- Breach of CBA no. 24 could carry a fine of up to EUR300-3 000 per worker affected, subject to an overall maximum of EUR300 000.
- Instead of criminal penalties, the authorities could impose administrative fines of EUR150 to EUR1 500 per affected worker, up to a maximum of EUR150 000.
- Under the Renault Act it is also possible to force companies to reimburse any government support in the event of noncompliance with the information and consultation procedure. To our knowledge, only the Flemish government has to date promulgated legislation in this respect.

Collective Dismissal Indemnity

[354] Collective dismissal is construed as meaning any dismissal for economic or technical reasons that, over an uninterrupted period of sixty days, affects a certain number of workers representing at least 10% of the effective average workforce for the calendar year preceding dismissal. There is a collective dismissal in the case of companies employing between twenty and fifty-nine workers where at least six workers are dismissed in the said period of sixty days.

[355] Hence, the notion of a collective dismissal is defined differently in the provisions relating to the collective dismissal indemnity compared to those relating to the obligation to comply with the preliminary information and consultation procedure. This means that, in certain (exceptional) cases, the employer can be bound to pay a collective dismissal indemnity for collective dismissal without being obliged to follow the preliminary information and consultation procedure with the workers' representatives. The following table clarifies the situation:

Minimum Number of Dismissals

Number of Workers	*Application of the Information and Consultation Procedure*	*Entitlement to a Collective Dismissal Indemnity*
Less than 20	*Not applicable*	*Not applicable*
20 to 59	*If at least 10 workers are dismissed*	*if at least 6 workers are dismissed*
60 to 99	*If at least 10 workers are dismissed*	*if at least 10% of the workers are dismissed*
100 to 299	*if at least 10% of the workers are dismissed*	*if at least 10% of the workers are dismissed*
300 or more	*If at least 30 workers are dismissed*	*if at least 10% of the workers are dismissed*

Amount of the Collective Dismissal Indemnity

[356] In the event of a collective dismissal, the employer can be liable to pay a collective dismissal indemnity to the workers (both blue and white-collar workers). Compensation is calculated in accordance with a complex formula, being half the difference between a net reference salary before dismissal and the unemployment benefits to which the workers are entitled. The net reference pay corresponds to gross monthly pay, with a ceiling of EUR3 273 (this amount was applicable as of 1 June 2016 and is regularly subject to indexation).

[357] This collective dismissal indemnity is payable to workers for a maximum of four months. However, where the dismissal notice period exceeds three months, each month in excess thereof reduces this four-month period by one month. In other words, the four-month maximum period for which collective dismissal indemnity is due is reduced by one month for each month of notice (or indemnity in lieu of notice) in excess of three which is given under the normal rules governing the termination of employment contracts. Thus, workers with basic notice periods of seven months or more will not be entitled to any collective dismissal indemnity. The following table illustrates this rule:

Length of Notice Period	*Period for Which the Collective Dismissal Indemnity Can Be Due*
four months	*three months*
five months	*two months*
six months	*one month*
seven months	*nil*

[358] It should be noted that the collective dismissal indemnity cannot be aggregated with the aforementioned closure indemnity, or with the protection indemnity due in cases of wrongful dismissal of protected workers.

Reintegration Indemnity and the Establishment of an Employment Action Groups

[359] All undertakings carrying out a collective dismissal must set up an employment action group or must join a permanent employment action group established by the subregional unemployment authorities, if they have done so.

[360] The employment action group, which includes a representative of the employer, at least one trade union and the subregional unemployment authority, organizes training sessions and assistance for the workers dismissed in the framework of a collective dismissal, aimed at assisting the workers in finding a new suitable job. The nature and duration of this assistance is determined by negotiation between the employer and the trade unions, except that the employment action group must always at least offer outplacement assistance which at least meets the conditions laid down in the CBA no. 82 (some worker categories defined by law are not eligible for outplacement guidance).

[361] A reintegration indemnity is a payment that replaces three or six months of the notice period or the period covered by the indemnity in lieu of notice, depending on the age of the worker concerned. Eligible workers aged under 45 will receive a reintegration indemnity equal to three month's pay while eligible workers aged 45 or over will receive a reintegration indemnity equal to six month's pay. Only workers meeting specific conditions defined by law will be eligible for payment of a reintegration indemnity.

[362] During the period for which the reintegration indemnity is paid, the recipient can participate in training and assistance offered by the employment action group, aiming at assisting the affected workers tin their search for a new suitable job. If a reintegration indemnity is due, it is not possible to terminate the employment contract by serving a notice period unless the worker is entitled to a notice period exceeding three or six months (depending on the relevant period of payment of the reintegration indemnity). In that case, it is still possible to have the worker perform part of the notice period, provided the last three or six months are replaced by reintegration indemnity.

Transfer of a Part of a Business as a Going Concern

[363] The principle that employment contracts should be maintained in the event of a change of employer by reason of a contractual transfer of an undertaking and, as a corollary, the prohibition against dismissal have been transposed into CBA no. 32 *bis* of 7 June 1985, which was made binding by the Royal Decree of 25 July 1985. It incorporates into Belgian law the principles set out in EC Directive 2001/23 of 12 March 2001.

Scope

[364] There is a contractual transfer of an undertaking or part of an undertaking, and therefore application of CBA no. 32 *bis*, where the following three conditions are met:

(i) the transfer must effect a change of employer. The CBA's provisions are not triggered where the transaction (a reorganization, takeover bid, concentration of undertakings, etc.) does not alter the legal identity of the employer; and
(ii) the transfer has to take place in a contractual framework, although there is no requirement for a contract between the transferor and the transferee directly. The transfer may result from an assignment, a merger, an absorption, the incorporation of a company or a change in the legal form of the undertaking; and
(iii) there must be a transfer of an undertaking or part of an undertaking. This notion is construed very broadly. 'Part of an undertaking' is interpreted as a collection of assets that are sufficiently important and that, being technically interlinked, are united by virtue of a certain production process and are suited to function autonomously. The transfer may be vertical (a homogenous, easily identifiable ensemble, such as a division or department) or horizontal (an ensemble of elements belonging to various departments of the undertaking). It is also necessary that the economic entity transferred should subsist or still exist and retain its identity. Such is generally the case where the economic operation is pursued or taken over by the new employer with identical, or at least similar, activities.

Maintaining the Rights of the Workforce

[365] CBA no. 32 *bis* requires the rights and obligations of the transferor (the former employer) in resulting from the employment contracts existing on the date of transfer to be transferred to the transferee (the new employer), with the exception of the workers' rights to old-age, invalidity or survivors' benefits under supplementary schemes outside the statutory Belgian social security schemes which were not concluded in a CBA applicable to the transferred business.

[366] An employer that takes over part of an undertaking is therefore obliged also to takeover the existing employment contracts (defined in the broad sense, i.e., individual employment contracts, terms of CBAs which were incorporated into the individual employment contracts, company policies, work regulations, etc.) of the personnel working for the part of the undertaking that is being transferred, and to maintain the rights and obligations of the employment contracts for the workers (e.g., working conditions, pay, seniority, benefits granted to the workforce, etc.).

[367] In this respect, it should be noted that both the old and the new employers are obliged to pay the amount due to the workers under the existing contracts, at the time of the changeover from one employer to the next. The new employer is therefore bound for the future, and is also bound, jointly and severally with the old employer, to pay debts existing as at the date of transfer.

Protection Against Dismissal

[368] CBA no. 32 *bis* prohibits the transferor and transferee from dismissing the transferor's workers for other reasons than serious cause, except if their dismissal is justified by economic, technical or organizational reasons. Workers can however be dismissed for serious cause or for economic, technical or organizational reasons entailing changes in the field of employment. The economic, technical or organizational reasons relied upon may be the less-than-flourishing financial health of the undertaking, the necessity for absorption to allow the undertaking to retain its position in the market, or the impossibility of redeploying the workers who have been or are about to be transferred once the employer has reviewed all the options available to the company, such as allocating the worker to another job compatible with his or her qualifications.

[369] In order to be unlawful, the dismissal must be effected before or after the date of transfer, but within such a period that the two events (dismissal and transfer) have to be regarded as linked. Although there is no fixed limit in this regard, it is fairly unlikely that the Belgian employment courts would consider a dismissal effected outside a period of around six to nine months before or after the transfer as being linked to the transfer. Thus, it is for the employment court to assess whether the contract termination is lawful in the light of the requirements of CBA no. 32 *bis*. If the court considers the dismissal to be unlawful, because it is linked to the transfer and not justified by economic, technical or organizational reasons, it will order the employer to pay not only compensation in lieu of notice but also damages for abusing its rights or for 'flagrantly unreasonable dismissal', as defined by law (in the CBA no. 109).

[370] Attention should also be given to the possibility that a transfer of undertaking may in specific circumstances result in constructive dismissal, for instance if the employer unilaterally has to modify the duties or the function of the worker substantially or if the place of work is unilaterally changed. In those circumstances, termination of the employment contract is regarded as due to an act by the employer, who must pay compensation in lieu of notice.

A Share in the Capital

[371] Finally, it is not unusual for the purchaser to offer the directors, existing or newly appointed, or certain workers shares or stock options in the capital of the company they are to manage. The workers can therefore acquire stock options in their business at a price fixed in advance (known as the 'exercise' or 'strike price') for a certain period. The options are incorporated into a scheme, i.e., the employer (or its parent company) determines the beneficiaries under the scheme, the criteria and the conditions for its application, and the terms of exercise of the stock option scheme. The stock options can be in the company for which the beneficiaries work or shares issued by an affiliated company, generally the group parent company. The worker will receive a benefit if there is a difference when exercising the options between the value of the share and the cost borne by the worker.

[372] By application of sections 41-47 of the Taxes Act of 26 March 1999, provided certain conditions are met, the benefit resulting from the allocation of a stock option is subject to personal income tax at fixed rates in the hands of the holder at the time the option is awarded. It is therefore the initial value of the option (i.e., the amount of the bonus valued on a notional basis) that determines what the taxable benefit is. From a tax point of view, the option can be accepted in writing up to the 60th day following the date of the offer, even if exercise of the option is subject to conditions precedent or subsequent. In the absence of written acceptance of the stock options within this period, the beneficiary is deemed to refuse the offer. Section 43 of the Act of 26 March 1999 lays down how to calculate the value of the taxable benefit.

[373] The tax is final. In principle, this benefit is not subject to social security contributions.

[374] In relation to shares, the Act of 22 May 2001 on worker participation in the capital and profits of companies provides that workers can be awarded shares exempt from social security contributions and taxed at a reduced rate of 15%, provided numerous conditions are met, notably the fact that the incentive scheme must be incorporated into a CBA.

[375] The notion of 'remuneration' used for the calculation of social security contributions requires that it be 'borne by the employer'. Hence, no social security contributions are due on forms of worker incentive that are not directly or indirectly financed by the employer. Further, to be exempt from social security contributions, the employer cannot be directly or indirectly involved in any way in the incentive granting procedure (e.g., incentive not granted via intermediary of the employer's payroll). The most recent version of the guidelines for employers issued by the National Office for Social Security nevertheless creates doubt as to the precise scope of this principle.

[376] Setting up a stock option scheme requires compliance with certain formalities, especially with regard to securities law (public offers to investors are strictly regulated and must be authorized by the CBFA on the basis of a prospectus relating to the contemplated transaction).

[377] A number of problems raised by stock option schemes in relation to employment law remain unsettled, notably the impact of stock options on the calculation basis of the indemnity in lieu of notice. In its judgment of 4 February 2002, the Court of Cassation nonetheless ruled that a stock option constitutes a possibility to obtain profit by exercising the stock option, and that the value of this possibility should be taken into account for the calculation of compensation in lieu of notice. The Court went on to say that only the value of this possibility should be included, irrespective of whether or not the worker has been able to exercise the stock options and irrespective of the eventual profits made by exercising the stock options. While this judgment nevertheless clearly established the principles in this respect, employment courts and employment appeal courts have subsequently developed contradictory case law on how the value of stock options should be determined for the purpose of calculating the indemnity in lieu of notice. This should therefore be assessed on a case-by-case basis, based on the type of stock option granted to the worker.

[378] The relationship between the benefit flowing from a stock option agreement and employment law also arises in relation to the following issues:

(d) Unilateral amendment of the scheme by the employer: if the benefit does not form part of the contractually agreed remuneration, the stock option plan may, under certain conditions, be cancelled at any time and confers no rights for the future. The employer is only deemed to have constructively dismissed the worker if it unilaterally amends an essential element of the employment contract. Although pay is obviously an essential element of the contract, it is generally, albeit not unanimously, accepted that an employer can stipulate in the employment contract that variable remuneration or profit sharing does not constitute a vested right in relation to future periods of employment. Adding such clause could strengthen the employer's position when arguing that the worker did not obtain an acquired right to payment of the said benefit or incentive. That being said, the worker could nevertheless still validly claim having acquired a customary right to payment thereof, if the relevant benefit or incentive was consistently granted to him over a substantial period. At the time the stock option scheme is set up, a clause may be incorporated stating that it constitutes an *ex gratia* benefit and does not create any vested right for the future and, possibly, that it is limited in time.

(e) Conditions linked to being in service: a stock option plan generally provides for the right to the shares to be forfeited in certain circumstances (dismissal for serious cause, etc.). If the benefit were to be regarded as pay, these circumstances would somehow have to be objective in nature. Such condition is under given circumstances accepted by case law, provided the stock option plan primarily intends to reward the worker's loyalty and length of service. If the stock option plan is primarily focussed on rewarding performance, though, the condition to be in service on the granting date will mostly be declared invalid by Belgian courts.

(f) Language rules: Finally, it should be borne in mind that Belgian law strictly regulates what language is to be used in communications between worker and employer. Depending on the facts, communications should be made in Dutch, French or German, failing which they may be void and unenforceable towards the workers. Nullity nevertheless does not affect the rights of the workers involved, hence they could still claim entitlements resulting from the plan (even if it would be unenforceable due to noncompliance with the statutory language requirements). However, the Belgian legislation on the use of languages does in principle not apply to the relationship between an worker and any third person, for instance where the parent company of the employer might administer a stock option scheme.

PROCEDURAL FORMALITIES

[379] The Companies Code lays down the procedural and disclosure formalities applicable to mergers, divisions, simple share acquisitions, takeover bids and transfers of controlling interests. These requirements are discussed in further detail below.

Mergers and Splits

Merger by Way of Absorption

[380] By law, mergers by way of absorption (sections 693-704, Companies Code) require transfer of all the assets of the absorbed company in exchange for a transfer of shares in the absorbing company to the shareholders of the absorbed company. The exchange of assets and shares must be 'fair', i.e., at par value or including a supplement of a maximum of one-tenth of the value of the shares. Accordingly, payment of a higher premium enables any person interested to initiate legal action and challenge the merger decision. The first step to be taken is that the boards of directors of each of the companies involved prepare a special report, called the 'merger proposal', in which the purposes and the terms and conditions of the proposed merger are explained. This report must be filed with the clerk of the commercial court and published in accordance with section 74 or 75 of the Companies Code at least six weeks before the date of the shareholders' meeting that is to take the final decision on the merger. Even if the absorbing and absorbed companies prepare the same merger proposal, two individual proposals still have to be filed. The board of directors of each of the companies involved also has to draw up a detailed written report which, amongst others, explains and justifies, from a e legal and economic point of view, the desirability, conditions, terms and consequences of the merger, the methods used to determine the exchange ratio of the shares, the difficulties that may have been encountered and the proposed exchange ratio. If all shareholders and holders of other voting rights in both companies agree, this report is not required. The board of directors of each company must inform its shareholders' meeting and the governing bodies of the other companies involved in the merger if there is to be a significant change in its assets after the merger proposal and before the final merger decision. Major changes mean any event having an influence on the net assets of one of the companies in question, such a sale of its crown jewels or the accounting of doubtful debtors. The shareholders and holders of other voting rights in both companies can unanimously decide that this additional information is not required. In addition, a report has to be made by a chartered auditor (commissaire-reviseur/commissaris-revisor) or a registered accountant testifying to the accuracy of the accounting procedures used in the transaction. Again the shareholders and holders of other voting rights in both companies can unanimously agree that this report is not required.

[381] The shareholders' meetings of all the companies concerned are responsible for taking the final merger decision. If a public limited liability company (SA/NV) already owns at least 90%, but not all, of the shares of the target company, the merger does not have to be approved by the shareholders' meeting of the absorbing company if certain conditions are met (section 699(6), Companies Code). Special provisions guarantee shareholder protection, especially in the field of the full disclosure of information. It is worth noting that even holders of non-voting shares have a right to vote on adoption of the merger (section 481(3°), Companies Code). Immediately after adoption of the merger, the shareholders' meeting of the absorbing company must decide on the necessary amendments to its articles of association; if it fails to do so, the merger proposal may be nullified. The minutes of the shareholders' meeting of each participating company must be embodied in a notarial deed. Furthermore, these decisions are subject to specific publication requirements in order for them to become binding vis-à-vis third parties.

[382] The board of directors of the absorbed company completes all accounting formalities for the period up to the point of the merger. The financial statements of the absorbed company as at the effective date of the merger must be approved by the shareholders meeting of the absorbing company. The shareholders' meeting of the absorbing company also relieves the board of directors and the statutory auditor of the absorbed company of any liability relating to performance of their duties before the merger. Within two months after publication of the merger resolutions, creditors of any of the merged companies whose debts existed prior to the merger or is subject to a claim against any of the merged companies introduced in court or through arbitration complaint before the shareholders' meeting deciding on the merger can demand warranties before the commercial court. Any contractual provisions to the contrary are deemed by law to be void.

Merger by Way of Constitution of a New Company

[383] This form of merger (sections 705-718, Companies Code) is subject to the same limitation of the one-tenth supplementary payment as under the previous method. The new company, whatever its legal form, must be constituted by notarial deed, which contains the board's merger proposal and the report of the statutory auditor. As in the case of a merger by absorption, the merger proposal must be filed with the clerk of the commercial court and published in accordance with section 74 or 75 of the Companies Code six weeks before the date of the shareholders' meeting and the shareholders' meeting has to decide on the merger proposal. The same meeting has to resolve on adoption of the articles of association of the new company, and to incorporate it; again, if it fails to do so, the merger proposal may be nullified. The various resolutions of the shareholders' meeting must be published in compliance with the Companies Code.

Other Operations Equivalent to Merger

[384] The following operations deemed to be equivalent to mergers (sections 676-677, Companies Code) are also deemed by law to be subject to the regime referred to above:

- winding-up of a company and transfer of all its assets to another company that already holds 100% of the shares and other voting securities of the wound-up company;
- winding-up of a company and transfer of all its assets to another company, if 100% of the shares or other voting securities of the wound-up company are held by the company to which the assets are transferred or by third parties who hold such shares or voting securities for the account of the latter company.
- mergers falling under section 671 of the Companies Code that are implemented without all the transferor entities ceasing to exist.

[385] These transactions have the following characteristics:

- all shares of the company making the transfer disappear from the balance sheet of the company benefiting from the transfer and are replaced by its net assets.

Split to Absorb a Company

[386] Splits by way of absorption are covered by sections 728-741 of the Companies Code. As under section 671 of the Companies Code, a transfer of all of the assets of the split company may be carried out in consideration for the issue to its shareholders of a number of shares in the absorbing company amounting to the par value of such assets plus a maximum of one-tenth of that value. Any higher payment makes the transfer voidable. As with the merger procedure, a split starts with split proposals, to be drawn up by the board of directors of the company to be split and by the board of directors of each of the absorbing companies. Each split proposal must be filed with the clerk of the commercial court and published in accordance with section 74 or 75 of the Companies Code at least six weeks before the date of the shareholders' meeting that is to decide on the split. The proposal must include a substantial report from the board explaining the asset situation of the split company, all the reasons why the split is being undertaken and the justification for the exchange ratio. The same exception as in the case of mergers applies. This proposal is therefore very similar to that required in relation to mergers. However, the two proposals are distinguished by the obligation, which applies only to divisions, of stating in the report the exact split of shares to the members of the company to be divided and the split of net assets to be transferred between the absorbing companies. Any major change in the assets of the split company up to the date of the shareholders' meeting has to be notified to the board of directors of each absorbing company. In addition, an official statement has to be made by a chartered auditor (commissaire-reviseur/commissaris-revisor) or a registered accountant, unless all shareholders and holders of other voting rights unanimously waive this requirement.

[387] At least one month before the shareholders' meeting, each shareholder of the companies involved has the right to examine these two reports, as well as the annual reports for the three preceding years of each of the companies involved.

[388] The shareholders' meetings of all the companies involved must pass resolutions on final adoption of the split proposal. Again, even holders of non-voting shares may participate in the ballot (section 481, Companies Code). At the same meeting, the shareholders of the absorbing companies also have to pass resolutions on the amendment of their articles of association; if they fail to do so, the proposal to split the company may be nullified. The minutes of the shareholders' meetings of each company have to be incorporated in a notarial deed. Each resolution of the shareholders' meeting of each company is subject to publication, as required by the Companies Code.

Split to Set Up a New Company

[389] Splits by way of constitution of new companies are covered by sections 742-757 of the Companies Code. As in the previous cases of mergers and splits, this type of transaction is also subject to the one-tenth premium limit; in case of payment exceeding one-tenth of the value of the shares the transaction may be nullified. Each new company must be constituted by notarial deed, whatever the legal form of the company. The decisions of the shareholders' meetings of each of the companies involved are the same mutatis mutandis as in the case of a merger by constitution of a new company as referred to above. Again, they are subject to all publication requirements under company law. Where the commercial court holds that, according to the criteria referred to in the Companies Code, the resolution to split is void, this automatically results in the nullity of the newly formed companies.

Combined Split Transaction

[390] Splits by way of absorption and constitution of new companies are covered by section 758 of the Companies Code. This kind of split is subject to the combined regimes of both types of transactions discussed above.

Summary of the Merger Process

[391] The merger process can be summarized as follows:

(a) preparation of financial statements of the absorbed company;
(b) merger proposal drawn up by the board of directors of each of the companies taking part in the merger;
(c) filing of merger proposal with the clerk of the commercial court and publication by each of the companies taking part in the merger, at least six weeks before the general meetings called to discuss it;
(d) detailed written report by the management on the merger and the situation as regards assets and liabilities, if required;
(e) report of the statutory auditor, if required;
(f) additional report by the boards of directors of each of the companies in the event of a substantial change between the time of the merger proposal and the general meeting, unless the shareholders and holders of other voting rights have waive their right to this additional information;
(g) possible consultation of the merger proposal, the reports and the annual accounts for the last three years (plus an intermediate report if the current year has been running for more than six months) of each of the companies involved, at least one month before the general meeting called to discuss it;
(h) general meeting of each of the companies involved (except under certain strict conditions), with a quorum of one-half and a majority of three-quarters of the votes (section 558, Companies Code);

(i) for each of the companies involved, notarial deed containing the minutes of the general meeting that resolves to proceed with the merger together with the merger proposal and the reports;
(j) filing with the clerk of the commercial court and publication in the supplements to the official gazette (Moniteur belge/Belgische Staatsblad) of the deeds relating to the merger, simultaneously for all the companies taking part in the transaction.

[392] The same procedure is followed *mutatis mutandis* in the case of a split.

Nullity of the Merger or Split

[393] Sections 688-689 of the Companies Code provide for two special cases where a merger or split will be void:

(a) where the operation fulfils the essential characteristics laid down by law but the premium is greater than one-tenth of the par value of the shares allotted or, where there is no par value, the accounting par; and
(b) if the transaction is not set down in a notarial deed.

[394] Moreover, the law refers to nullity in terms of a general provision on the nullity of general meeting resolutions. Section 64 of the Companies Code particularly covers the following cases:

(a) a formal irregularity impinging on the general meeting's decision, provided the plaintiff proves that the irregularity could have affected the decision;
(ii) breach of the procedural rules governing general meetings or deliberation of an item not contained on the agenda in the presence of fraudulent intent;
(iii) excess of powers or abuse of power impinging upon the decision;
(iv) the exercise of voting rights in spite of bring suspended by virtue of a statutory provision not contained in the Companies Code such that, had these rights not been exercised unlawfully, the quorum or majority requirements for the general meeting's decisions would not have been met;
(v) any other cause provided for in the Companies Code.

Cross-Border Mergers

[395] Until recently, there were no Community regulations governing mergers between companies established in different Member States. To be valid, such mergers have to be effected between two companies established in two states in which the cross-border merger mechanism is provided for by statute. In addition, this type of merger might give rise to very serious financial consequences and entail recourse to alternative legal mechanisms leading to an element of legal uncertainty. It was in this context that it was felt there was a need to legislate on such transactions at a European level.

[396] In force since 15 December 2005, Directive 2005/56/EC on cross-border mergers of limited liability companies was adopted by the Council and the European

Parliament on 26 October 2005. The aim of this directive was to facilitate cross-border mergers between limited liability companies of the European Union by reducing their costs and improving the transparency of such transactions. The measure required to be transposed into the legal systems of the Member States no later than 15 December 2007. In Belgium, it was the Financial Arrangements (Miscellaneous Provisions) Act of 8 June 2008 that transposed the directive by introducing a new Title V bis into Book XI of the Companies Code.

Directive 2005/56/EC and the New Title V bis of Book XII of the Companies Code

[397] The procedure set up by Directive 2005/56/EC is very close to that which currently governs mergers between companies established in Belgium. First, the boards of directors of each of the merging companies have to prepare a joint cross-border merger proposal, which must contain certain obligatory elements laid down by Directive 2005/56/EC. These same bodies must then prepare the report on that proposal intended for the shareholders or members of the companies in the merger and their workforce. An independent expert's report also has to be drawn up to analyse the merger. Once these documents have been drawn up, the general meetings of each of the merging companies then have to vote on whether to approve the joint cross-border merger proposal.

[398] In relation to oversight of the legality of the merger, Directive 2005/56/EC distinguishes verification of the procedure applying to each of the merging companies from oversight of consummation of the cross-border merger as such. Each Member State designates, first, the competent authority to verify the legality of the merger procedure, in so far as it falls under the national laws of the company. Before the merger takes place, a certificate attesting to the fact that these formalities have been duly adhered to therefore has to be issued by the authorities in each of the Members States where the merging companies are established.

[399] Each Member State designates the competent authority to oversee implementation of the cross-border merger. These authorities only have jurisdiction in so far as the merger falls under their national legislation. In this regard, Directive 2005/56/EC states that the applicable law is the law of the State of establishment of the company resulting from the merger. The date of consummation of the merger is fixed by the law of that same State.

[400] The main principles laid down in Directive 2005/56/EC should be borne in mind at all times. These are as follows:

- Enshrinement of the so-called 'distributive' method, in terms of which 'a company taking part in a cross-border merger shall comply with the provisions and formalities of the national law to which it is *subject*' (Article 4(1)(b) of the Directive). As a consequence, there is no cumulative application of the national laws of the various companies taking part in the transaction. Each company involved in the operation will apply 'its' national law as regards, in particular, the decision-making process, the protection of creditors, bondholders and holders of securities or shares, as well as the workforce as regards rights of participation organized by the directive. This 'distributive' method is now laid down in section 113 of the Belgian Private International Law Code.

- Alignment of the cross-border merger regime with that governing domestic mergers. Unless Directive 2005/56/EC provides otherwise, each company taking part in a cross-border merger, and any third party having an interest, continues to be subject to the provisions and formalities of national law such as would apply to a domestic merger. Accordingly, in relation to Belgium's Companies Code, that means that Title II ('the rules governing mergers, divisions and equivalent operations') of Book XI ('corporate reorganizations') also applies to the new Title V bis ('special rules on cross-border mergers and equivalent operations'), unless there should be provision to the contrary in that latter title.
- Enshrinement of the principle of the universal transfer of net assets, which characterizes domestic mergers.
- Priority given to legal certainty over the rights of members and third parties. The merger only takes effect *inter alia* after verification of the form of the joint merger proposal on a date fixed by the law of the Member State under which the absorbing company falls. Furthermore, a cross-border merger that has not come into effect can no longer be held to be void.
- The desire to reduce transaction costs (by simplifying the procedure), in order to open up the possibilities to SMEs. This desire is translated in particular by the facility introduced by Directive 2005/56/CE enabling companies involved in a merger to designate a joint independent expert and for the members unanimously to resolve to dispense with that report.
- Special rules relative to the workers of the companies involved. These rules are particularly an expression of the desire to ensure better information for the workers, and so the merger proposal must make express mention of 'the likely effects of the cross-border merger on *employment* (Article 5(d) of Directive 2005/56/EC). Likewise, the report by the board of directors of each of the companies involved must be made available to the workers or their representatives (Article 7 of Directive 2005/56/EC). Broadly inspired by the rules governing European companies, the provisions of Article 16 of Directive 2005/56/EC enshrine a number of measures relative to worker participation in cross-border mergers.

[401] Before Directive 2005/56/EC came into force, the validity of cross-border mergers had already been confirmed by a decision of the Court of Justice on 13 December 2005, at least in principle. In addition, as regards Belgium, even before the transposition of Directive 2005/56/EC, there was nothing in the Companies Code that seemed to stand in the way of a merger involving a foreign company.

[402] As stated above, Directive 2005/56/EC was transposed into Belgian law by the Financial Arrangements (Miscellaneous Provisions) Act of 8 June 2008 (official gazette, 16 June 2008), and section 77 introduced into Book XI of the Companies Code (entitled 'Corporate Reorganisations') a new Title V bis called 'Special rules on cross-border mergers and equivalent operations'. These provisions came into force on 26 June 2008.

[403] In relation to tax, the Act of 11 December 2008 amended the Income Tax Code with a view to transposing Directive 90/434/EEC of 23 July 1990 on the common system of taxation applicable to mergers, divisions, transfers of assets and exchanges of shares concerning companies of different Member States.

[404] As regards the scope of Directive 2005/56/EC, it is only applicable to merger operations, to the exclusion of divisions, contributions or transfers of lines of business or universal transfers of assets involving companies of different Member States. It therefore covers three different types of operations:

- merger by absorption;
- merger by incorporation of a new company;
- merger by absorption of a wholly owned subsidiary (an operation equated to a merger because it does not entail the allotment of shares by the beneficiary company). These mergers were previously known in French as 'silent' or 'English' mergers.

[405] On this matter, Title V bis of Book XI of the Companies Code dealing with cross-border mergers and equivalent operations merely refers to sections 671, 672 and 676 of the Companies Code on domestic mergers. There are therefore no specific definitions of these operations.

[406] Article 1 of Directive 2005/56/EC provides that it applies to mergers of 'limited liability companies formed in accordance with the law of a Member State and having their registered office, central administration or principal place of business within the Community, provided at least two of them are governed by the laws of different Member States'.

[407] For the directive to apply, some part of the operation therefore has to be 'cross-border' in nature, i.e., a merger between companies, at least two of which fall under the law of different Member States. The ruling criterion is a general criterion of falling under the laws of different Member States (without express reference to registered office or principal place of business or other decisive rule under the lex societatis). The 'principal place of business' criterion will be applicable under Belgian law to determine the law applying to the company resulting from the merger (section 110, Private International Law Code). Otherwise, it must be 'Community' companies that are involved, in the sense that each of the companies whose amalgamation is proposed have to have its registered office, its central administration or its principal place of business within the Community. This gives one to wonder why the criterion here is not that of the companies in question falling under the laws of the Member States. Furthermore, what about a company incorporated in one Member State applying the doctrine of incorporation to determine the lex societatis (such as the Netherlands) and thus falling under the law of a Member State but having its principal place of business in a third State, outside the Community?

[408] Unfortunately, the Companies Code does not defined how 'cross-border merger' is to be construed. This omission raises a number of questions regarding the geographical ambit of Title V bis of Book XI of the Code: first, is it to be determined on the basis of the provisions of Directive 2005/56/EC or is it to be interpreted as being broader? Although the directive is not of direct 'horizontal' effect, Belgian law nevertheless has to be interpreted in conformity with European law and the directive. It follows that only operations meeting the criteria set forth in Directive 2005/56/EC will be subject to the provisions of Title V bis of Book XI of the Code which is intended to transpose it. Other cross-border mergers should be carried out in accordance with the 'ordinary law' governing mergers. However, since there is no provision in Title V bis of Book XI of the Companies Code that limits the 'territorial' ambit of that Title to operations under the directive, it might be permissible to interpret it broadly, as being liable also to apply to operations between 'Belgian' companies and 'non-Community' companies. In this regard, intervention by Belgium's lawmakers would be welcome so as to avoid any misconstruction.

[409] Then, one might wonder as to what provisions apply to mergers between a company under Belgian law endowed with legal personality and a company falling under foreign law where the operation does not meet the territorial criteria laid down in the directive. The absence of common Community rules for determining the lex societatis does not make the situation an easy one.

[410] As regards relevant companies, the provisions of Article 2 of Directive 2005/56/EC provides that it applies to all 'limited liability companies' within the meaning of Community law. According to the recitals to the proposal of directive to the European Parliament and the Council on cross-border mergers of limited liability companies *'limited liability companies are characterised by the fact that they enjoy legal personality and have separate corporate assets that alone fulfil the debts of the company'*. Under Belgian law, the entities in question are the public limited liability company (société anonyme/naamloze vennootschap), the partnership limited by shares (société en commandite par actions/commanditaire vennootschap), the private limited liability company (société privée à responsabilité limitée/besloten vennootschap met beperkte aansprakelijkheid) and the limited cooperative (société cooperative à responsabilité limitée/*coöperatieve* vennootschap met beperkte aansprakelijkheid). Belgian law has not made use of the option allowed under the directive of not applying it to cooperative companies. Hence, unlimited forms of doing business, like general partnerships (société en nom collectif/vennootschap onder firma), are excluded from the law's scope. As for mixed forms of doing business such as limited partnerships (société en commandite simple/gewone commanditaire vennootschap), their status is uncertain. Intervention by Europe's lawmakers would therefore be welcome in this regard to avoid any legal uncertainty.

[411] The scope of the Belgian legislation is somewhat broader. It is applicable to all forms of doing business endowed with legal personality that are able to merge at a national level. The following are nonetheless excluded from the ambit of Title V bis of Book XI of the Companies Code:

- open-end investment funds (SICAVs/BEVEKs) falling under sections 10 and 14 of the Act of 20 July 2004 on certain forms of collective management of investment portfolios;
- companies, partnerships and cooperatives in liquidation.

[412] Companies in insolvency may take part in a cross-border merger provided they have not already made a start on distributing assets to their shareholders.

Consideration for the Contribution: Rate of Balancing Payment

[413] Section 772/2 of the Companies Code provides that a cross-border merger is valid notwithstanding any balancing payment in cash exceeding one-tenth of the par value of the shares allotted to the company resulting from the cross-border merger or, failing a par value, of their accounting par, on condition that the legislation applying to at least one of the foreign companies allows this. Specifically, a balancing payment of over 10% is not in principle possible in Belgium unless the national legislation applicable to at least one of the foreign companies involved in the merger allows this. In this respect, it makes no difference whether the Belgian company is the absorbing or absorbed company. We would recall that, as far as domestic mergers are concerned, section 671 of the Companies Code limits the possibility of remunerating the contribution by according a balancing payment in cash unless it does not exceed one-tenth of the par value of the shares allotted or, failing a par value, of their accounting par.

Procedure

[414] Sections 772/6-772/14 of the Companies Code set out the procedure to be followed, which to a large extent is very similar to the procedure applying to domestic mergers.

[415] As in the case of domestic mergers, the board of directors of each of the merging companies have to draw up a 'joint cross-border merger proposal' containing the principal features of the transaction. The aims of this document are as follows:

- to reflect the results of the preliminary talks that must necessarily preface a merger;
- to inform the shareholders and third parties of the merger proposal;
- to serve as a basis for the preparatory procedures involving general meetings of shareholders of the companies involved in the merger, drawing up the reports of the experts and of the statutory auditors of the Companies involved and boards; and
- to permit the merger-control operations.

[416] According to Belgian law and Community law, a joint cross-border merger proposal is not binding on the companies involved either in terms of its principles or as to the operational procedures. Article 5 of Directive 2005/56/EC sets out the minimum items that must figure in the document. National legislatures and the officers of the companies concerned are free to add such other information as they deem appropriate. Under Belgian law, section 772/6 of the Companies Code sets forth these compulsory particulars. Apart from those already required in domestic merger proposals (sections 693 and 706 of the Companies Code), Belgian and European law do lay down additional information requirements, mainly owing to the cross-border nature of the operation. They particularly concern:

- the probable effects of the cross-border merger on jobs;
- the articles of association of the company resulting from the cross-border merger;

- information concerning the valuation of the assets and liabilities transferred to the company resulting from the cross-border merger;
- if appropriate, information on the procedures relative to worker involvement are laid down, in particular in respect of the definition of their rights of participation in the company resulting from the cross-border merger;
- the dates of the accounts of the merging companies as used to define the terms of the cross-border merger, or the tender report.

[417] Because the directive says nothing as to the form and language of the joint merger proposal, Belgian law allows it to be drawn up in the form of a notarial deed or of a private contract (section 772/6 of the Companies Code). By application of the national rules on the use of languages, it has to be written in French and/or Dutch and/or German. The same goes for the other documents relating to the merger.

[418] Under section 772/7 of the Companies Code, the Belgian companies involved must, within six weeks before the general meeting called to resolve on a cross-border merger, lodge the joint cross-border merger proposal at the registry of the commercial court in the judicial district where they have their respective registered offices, and arrange for a notice to be published in the schedules to the official gazette, in accordance with section 74 or 75 of the Companies Code.

[419] Finally, a number of criminal penalties are laid down in the Companies Code for failure to state the required particulars in the merger proposal (section 773(1°) Companies Code). Failure to adhere to the obligations in relation to publication and compulsory particulars can render the directors liable for breach of the Companies Code (section 528). They can also be liable to the shareholders of the company or companies wound up, on the basis of section 687 of the Companies Code. Nonetheless, the absence of the compulsory particulars cannot result in the merger operation being void. At most, the notary public may refuse to officiate in the context of double scrutiny of the legality of the merger (Articles 10 and 11 of Directive 2005/56/EC).

Report by the Management or Board

[420] In transposing Article 7 of Directive 2005/56/EC, section 772/8 of the Companies Code remains faithful to the existing rules on domestic mergers (section 694 of the Code). It requires the management or the board of directors of each company that merges to prepare a report explaining and justifying both the legal and the economic aspects of the cross-border merger and explaining its consequences for the shareholders, creditors and employees. Under Belgian law, this detailed, written report:

1. sets out the asset situation of the companies whose merger is proposed;
2. explains and justifies the economic and legal aspects such as:
   - the appropriateness of the cross-border merger, together with its terms and procedures;
   - its consequences for the shareholders, creditors and employees;
   - the methods followed in determining the share exchange ratio, the relative importance given to those methods, the values arrived at by each method, any difficulties encountered and the proposed exchange ratio.

[421] The report has to be made available to the shareholders and workers' representatives (or, where there are no representatives, the workers themselves) no later than one month before the date of the general meeting that is set to resolve on the merger proposal. Because this period also applies to the information to be given to the workers, the shareholders cannot give their unanimous consent to dispensing with this deadline, unlike the situation that occasionally occurs in domestic mergers.

Auditor's Report

[422] As in relation to a domestic merger, Article 8 of Directive 2005/56/EC provides that, for each company that merges, a report has to be drawn up by an independent expert. Section 772/9 of the Companies Code entrusts the task of independent expert to the statutory auditor, failing whom, a company auditor or external chartered accountant designated by the board of directors.

[423] The statutory auditor, company auditor or external chartered accountant must 'particularly state whether, in his opinion, the exchange ratio is relevant and reasonable'. This statement must at least:

- indicate 'the methods followed to determine the exchange ratio proposed' and 'whether these methods are appropriate in this case';
- 'state the values arrived at using each of these methods with an opinion being given on the relative importance placed on these methods in determining the value decided upon'; and
- indicate 'what particular valuation difficulties there might have been'.

[424] Section 772/9(1), fifth paragraph, of the Companies Code provides in this regard that the statutory auditor, company auditor or external chartered accountant has extended powers of investigation in relation to all the companies involved in the merger.

[425] In order to reduce merger expenses, it is possible to use the services of one or more joint experts for all the companies concerned to request the drawing up of a single written report containing a joint, consolidated assessment intended for the shareholders of all the companies involved in the merger. Appointment of the joint expert or experts is made by an administrative or judicial authority petitioned jointly by the companies concerned. This option, which is expressly provided for in Article 8(2) of Directive 2005/56/EC, is transposed in section 772/9(2) of the Companies Code and is far from unimportant for SMEs wanting to merge. Under Belgian law, it is the President of the commercial court who appoints these independent experts.

[426] The Companies Code provides for examination of the cross-border merger proposal by independent experts and for the experts' reports to be dispensed with. The decision naturally has to be taken unanimously by the Shareholders of each of the companies involved in the cross-border merger. Similarly, an operation equated to a cross-border merger does not need a single expert's report. However, the report drawn up by the board cannot be dispensed. This is no doubt explained by the fact that that report is intended for the information not only of the shareholders, but also of the workforce.

[427] If the directors fail to submit a special report accompanied by a report from the statutory auditor, a company auditor or a chartered account, they may be liable to criminal penalties under section 773(2°) of the Companies Code.

Approval by the Shareholders in General Meeting

[428] The Belgian rules governing the provisions and formalities for the decision-making process in relation to cross-border mergers are very similar to those governing domestic mergers. This part of the procedure includes notifying and informing the shareholders and approval by the general meeting.

[429] As regards notification and information of the shareholders, the only difference with domestic mergers is that, in order to limit the administrative expenses attendant on cross-border mergers, it is no longer required that a copy of the merger proposal and the reports provided for in sections 772/8 and 772/9 be sent to the holders of registered shares and persons fulfilling the formalities laid down by the articles of association to be admitted to general meetings.

[430] Section 772/10(1) of the Companies Code provides that the cross-border merger proposal and the report by the management or board and the auditor's report must be announced in the agenda of the general meeting called to vote on the cross-border merger proposal.

[431] Section 772/10(2) of the Companies Code sets forth the documents relative to all companies that merge, that any shareholder may inspect at least one month before the date of the general meeting called to vote on the cross-border merger proposal. In addition, as in the case of domestic mergers, 'an accounting statement drawn down to a date no more than three months prior to the date of the *cross-border* merger proposal' must be submitted to the shareholders 'where the *cross-border* merger proposal post-dates the end of the accounting period to which the last annual accounts pertain by six months or more'.

[432] Section 772/11 of the Companies Code provides that the general meetings of each of the companies merging have to vote on whether to approve the joint cross-border merger proposal. Belgian law thus does not take up the option offered by Directive 2005/56/EC of not requiring approval of the merger by the general meeting of the absorbing company if shareholders with a minimum holding in the absorbing company (maximum 5%) do not ask for such a meeting to be called. The quorum and majority conditions governing general meetings called to vote on a cross-border merger proposal are the same as for domestic mergers, i.e., the conditions laid down in section 558 of the Companies Code for amendment of the articles of association (a quorum of one half of the shares issued and a majority of three quarters of the votes).

[433] As regards operations equated to mergers, section 772/11(1), last paragraph, provides that the approval of the general meeting of the company 'taken over' is not required since, in that case, as set out in the recitals, that general meeting 'is a pure formality'. This exception is not, however, provided for as regards domestic mergers. Although for domestic mergers, in a public limited liability company (SA/NV) approval by the general meeting is not required if shareholders with a minimum holding in the absorbing company (maximum 5%) do not ask for such a meeting to be called (section 722(6) of the Companies Code).

[434] Section 772/11(2) of the Companies Code deals with possible alterations to the respective rights attaching to any classes of shares. This section reproduces the wording of section 699 of the Companies Code dealing with domestic mergers. The subsequent subsection requires the unanimous agreement of all the members for general partnerships (sociétés en nom collectif/vennootschappen onder firma), limited partnerships (sociétés en commandite simple/gewone commanditaire vennootschappen) and unlimited cooperatives (sociétés cooperatives à responsabilité *limitée/coöperatieve* vennootschappen met onbeperkte aansrapelijkheid).

[435] Immediately after the decision to carry out the cross-border merger, any amendments to the articles of association of the absorbing company, inclusive of any provisions amending its corporate objects, are decided on under the quorum and majority requirements laid down in the Companies Code. Otherwise, the merger decision is invalid (section 772/11(6), Companies Code).

[436] Section 772/11(5) of the Companies Code provides that the general meetings of each of the merging companies may make consummation of the cross-border merger subject to ratification by the shareholders of the special procedures relative to worker participation in the company resulting from the merger.

[437] As in the case of domestic mergers, with cross-border mergers, notwithstanding any contrary provision contained in the articles of association, the holders of non-voting shares nevertheless have a right to vote where the general meeting is to deliberate on the company's merger.

Double Control on Legality

[438] A double control on the legality of the transaction is exercised at two levels: at the level of each company taking part in the merger operation, on the one hand, and at the level of the company resulting from the merger, as regards realization of the merger, on the other hand.

[439] At the level of each company, the first control on legality is a preventive type of control pertaining to the legality of the internal merger procedure. In Belgium, section 772/12 of the Companies Code designates the officiating notary public as the competent control authority, since the minutes of the general meeting given the task of approving the merger are set down in a notarial deed. The notary public must certify the internal and external legality of the deeds required for the merger. He must without delay issue to each merging company falling under 'his' national legal system a certificate stating that the acts and formalities required prior to a cross-border merger as laid down in the Companies Code have without fail been duly carried out. If the statutory requirements have not been adhered to in their entirety, the notary public must refuse to officiate.

[440] Control of the entity resulting from the merger also falls under the authority of the officiating notary public in so far as the company resulting from the cross-border merger falls under his national legal system. Section 772/13 of the Companies Code provides that the officiating notary public has to verify that 'the merging companies have approved the joint cross-border merger proposal in identical terms and, if appropriate, that the procedures relating to worker participation have been set down in accordance with the provisions enacted by virtue of Article 16 of Directive 2005/56/EC'.

Coming into Effect of the Merger

[441] The date on which the notary public records that the cross-border merger has been consummated at the request of the merging companies upon presentation of the certificates and other documents constituting evidence of the transaction is the date on which the merger is deemed to come into effect. Naturally, where the merger involves the incorporation of a new company, the new company must also have already been incorporated.

[442] In relation to third parties, a cross-border merger will only be binding once the publication formalities have been gone through. Thus, the second paragraph of section 772/14 of the Companies Code provides that the notarial deed recording the cross-border merger and amending the articles of association of the absorbing company must be published in the supplements to the Belgian official gazette in accordance with the provisions of section 74 of the Companies Code. However, if these formalities are not carried out, it can still be evidenced that a third party against which it is wished the merger should be binding had previous knowledge of it. As regards the foreign company, procedures must still be enacted for notifying the effectiveness of the cross-border merger to the foreign register where the foreign company has filed its official deeds. Once this notification is received, the old register entry is to be struck.

[443] In order to ensure perfect security for all third parties having an interest in a cross-border merger in the various Member States concerned, section 772/5 of the Companies Code provides that a merger that has come into effect cannot be avoided. Therefore, the only available actions are:

- either a 'preventive' action prior to the general meeting, in order to get it suspended;
- or an action between the general meeting and the date the merger comes into effect;
- or actions for damages once the merger has come into effect.

[444] Under section 772/3 of the Companies Code, as from the date the cross-border merger comes into effect, the absorbed companies cease to exist, the members or shareholders of the wound-up companies become members or shareholders of the surviving companies (except in the case of an operation equated to a merger) and the entire assets and liabilities of each wound-up company are transferred to the surviving companies.

[445] Similarly, the rights and obligations of the merging companies arising under employment contracts or employment relations and existing on the date the cross-border takes effect are assigned to the company resulting from the merger, which is under an obligation to carry out all formalities resulting from these operations.

Contribution of a Line of Business or Contribution by Universal Transfer of Business Assets

General

[446] As mentioned above, the Companies Code also provides special regimes and specific rules for the contribution of a line of business and for the contribution by way of a universal transfer of assets. The regular transfer of a business is not covered by the legislation as such, so that the old principles and rules continue to apply to such transactions (*see also* above on the transfer of assets).

Definitions: Universal Transfer, Line of Business and Business

[447] Under section 678 of the Companies Code, a '*contribution by universal transfer of assets*' is effected where a company, without being wound up, transfers its entire property, both assets and liabilities, with the exclusion of its equity, to one or more existing or new companies, in exchange for remuneration comprising exclusively shares in the company or companies receiving such contributions.

[448] Under section 679 of the Companies Code, '*a contribution of a line of business*' is a transaction by which a company, without being wound up, transfers to another company a line of its business together with the liabilities and assets attaching thereto, in exchange for a remuneration comprising exclusively shares in the company receiving the contribution.

[449] Section 680 of the Companies Code further states that 'a *line of business*' means an ensemble that, from a technical point of view and seen organizationally, carries on an autonomous activity and is able to function by its own means.

[450] A business (fonds de commerce/handelszaak) is a collection of tangible and intangible assets united for a common end, i.e., the operation of a certain trade or business activity. It contains elements 'susceptible to retaining the customers' and 'of use to the fruitful organization and operation of the business'. The notion of a business is therefore less restricted than that of a line of business, '*which is more oriented towards production capacity and more restricted than that of a universal transfer of assets, which is broader and sometimes comprises several businesses*'. However, it can happen that a business coincides with a line of business so that its transfer is then subject to the rules relating to the contribution of a line of business, provided, of course, that the other conditions for such a transaction are fulfilled.

Company Contribution or Transfer

[451] The transfer of a line of business or a universal transfer of assets can be realized in the form of a company contribution or in the form of a transfer. A company contribution is remunerated by the issue to the contributing company of shares in the company receiving the contribution. A transfer is remunerated in cash or by an exchange of other property.

Contribution of a Line of Business or Contribution by Way of Universal Transfer of Business Assets

[452] The effects of a contribution of a line of business or a contribution by way of universal transfer of business assets as provided for under the statutory rules are transfer of the relevant assets and liabilities, allotment of shares to the contributing company and protection of third parties.

[453] However, the procedure under the Companies Code applies automatically only to universal transfers of business assets. Because the rules are optional in relation to contribution of a line of business for such transactions, the companies concerned can decide to exclude the statutory regime and, hence, render it non-binding vis-à-vis third parties as provided for by section 759 of the Companies Code.

The Transfer of Assets

[454] Under section 763 of the Companies Code, contribution of a line of business entails assignment of the entire assets and liabilities pertaining to the line of business being contributed. Contribution by way of a universal transfer of business assets entails transfer of the entire assets and liabilities of the contributing company. Such transfers are binding erga omnes by mere virtue of publication of an extract from the deed recording the contribution in the supplement to the Moniteur Belge/Belgisch Staatsblad (the Belgian Official Gazette), as provided by section 76 of the Companies Code, without any transfer formality being required for receivables and payables (section 765, Companies Code). The procedures for making the transfer binding upon debtors as laid down in section 1690 of the Civil Code therefore do not apply to this type of transfers. However, to ensure the enforceability of real rights, certain formalities must be completed as provided under the Mortgages Act.

Transfers of Shares to the Contributing Company

[455] A contribution of a line of business and a contribution by way of a universal transfer of business assets have the effect of allotting the shares in the beneficiary company to the contributing company. In this regard, the rules for contributions differ somewhat from those on mergers, since, first, the contributing company continues in existence whereas the absorbed company disappears in a merger and, second, it is the contributing company that receives the shares issued in remuneration of the contribution and not its shareholders.

Protection of Third Parties

[456] As with mergers and splits, and as is set out below, the creditors of the contributing company cannot oppose a contribution. However, they do have various ways of protecting their rights. The law makes provision for limited joint and several liability between the company receiving the contribution and the contributing company. Under

section 767 of the Companies Code the contributing company remains jointly and severally liable for debts that are certain and payable as of the date of contribution, that are transferred to a recipient company. The contributing company is equally jointly and severally liable for the debts which are subject to a claim against it introduced in court or through arbitration complaint before the shareholders' meeting deciding on the contribution. This liability of the contributing company is, however, limited to the net assets retained by the contributing company after the contribution, i.e., assets other than the property contributed. Third parties can assert unenforceability vis-à-vis them of the effect of the automatic transfer by operation of law where there has been a breach of sections 760 (preparation by the board of directors of each of the companies involved of a special report outlining the terms and conditions of the proposed contribution – *see* below) and 766 (failure to provide the security ordered by the president of the commercial court, as the case may be) of the Companies Code. In this respect, it must be pointed out that the creditors of the various companies in question can apply to the president of the commercial court for a security to be conferred on them (section 766, Companies Code). The president will determine whether there is cause to order such a security and, if so, will lay down its nature and the procedures therefore under the ordinary law, the creditors may file a creditors' action if the operation constitutes a fraud on their rights. They may file an urgent application to obtain an injunction suspending the resolutions adopted at a board meeting or at a shareholders meeting or suspending the meeting if the law has not been observed and if their rights are threatened. They may also invoke the directors' liability.

Procedure

[457] As in respect of mergers and divisions, a contribution of a line of business requires a special report, known as a 'proposal for the contribution of a line of business' to be drawn up by the board of directors of each of the companies participating in the contribution. This report must be filed with the clerk of the commercial court, for each of the companies participating, at least six weeks before the effective date of the contribution (section 760, Companies Code).

[458] Following the Act of 13 April 1995, a decision to contribute a line of business must, by virtue of section 761 of the Companies Code, result from a resolution to be adopted by the general meeting of shareholders of the contributing company, deciding under the special quorum and majority rules applicable for amendments to its articles of association, as set out in section 558 of the Companies Code, unless the articles of association of the company provide for more stringent requirements. The board of directors of the contributing company draws up a detailed written report setting out the property situations of the companies in question, explaining and stating the legal and economic reasons why the contribution is appropriate, together with its terms, procedures and consequences. A copy of the draft report is sent to the shareholders holding registered shares at least one month before the general meeting.

[459] In accordance with the ordinary rules, the capital of the company receiving the contribution has to be increased, either by a decision of the general meeting or by a resolution of the board of directors within the limits of the authorized capital. Therefore, an accountant's report must be drawn up, describing each contribution in kind, the valuation methods adopted and justifying the number of shares issued. The board of directors of the company receiving the contribution must also draw up a special report setting out, on the one hand, the benefits for the company resulting both from the contributions and from the capital increase proposed and, on the other hand, the reasons why it might possibly deviate from the conclusions of the accountant's report (section 602(1), Companies Code). These reports are filed with the clerk of the commercial court.

[460] Where the capital increase is decided on by the general meeting, as required by section 581 of the Companies Code, the mandatory reports are announced in the agenda. Copies of them are sent to the shareholders holding registered shares at the same time as the notice calling the meeting. They are also sent without delay to those persons who have fulfilled the formalities required by the articles of association to be admitted to the meeting.

Transfer of a Line of Business or Universal Transfer of Assets

[461] Under section 770 of the Companies Code, in the case of a transfer of a line of business or in the case of a universal transfer of assets remunerated in cash or by an exchange of other property, the parties may decide to benefit from a special regime providing for automatic transfer of all assets and liabilities by operation of the law. This special regime is broadly inspired by the rules applicable to the contribution of a line of business. Thus, in the case of a transfer of a line of business or in the case of a universal transfer of assets under the automatic transfer rules:

- a special report, called a 'proposal of transfer', has to be drawn up by the board of each of the companies involved and filed with the clerk of the commercial court at least six weeks before signature of the official deed of transfer;
- the transferee's decision is governed by its own articles of association;
- the principles of enforceability, the procedure for constituting sureties and the rules relating to joint and several liability also apply.

OBLIGATION TO DISCLOSE MAJOR SHAREHOLDINGS (TRANSPARENCY REGIME)

Introduction

[462] The parties to a 'merger and acquisition' transaction must not fail to address the questions of finance law that might result either from completion of a transaction falling within the definition of a public invitation to invest (appel public à l'épargne/ publiek beroep op het spaarweze*n*) or from the fact that the transferee company itself has made a public invitation to invest. The Belgian rules on this point have undergone far-reaching changes since 2006 and 2007. The main rules and regulations applying to 'merger and acquisition' transactions are as follows:

- the first chapter of the Act of 2 March 1989 on the public intimation of major holdings in stock market listed companies is no longer in force (see the Act of 2 May 2007 on the publicity of major holdings of issuers whose shares are admitted to trading on a regulated market and introducing miscellaneous provisions);
- the Act of 16 June 2006 on public offers of investment instruments and the admission of investment instruments to trading on regulated markets;
- the Act of 20 April 2007 on takeover bids;
- the Royal Decree of 27 April 2007 on takeover bids;
- the Act of 2 May 2007 on the publicity of major holdings of issuers whose shares are admitted to trading on a regulated market and introducing miscellaneous provisions;
- the Royal Decree of 14 November 2007 on obligations of issuers of financial instruments admitted to trading on a Belgian regulated market;
- the Royal Decree of 14 February 2008 on the publicity of major holdings.

[463] Some of the finance law consequences have been briefly mentioned above with regard to the study of acquisition and merger operations. Below is a brief analysis.

Disclosure of Interests in Shares

[464] The Act of 2 May 2007 on the publicity of major holdings of issuers whose shares are admitted to trading on a regulated market came into effect on partly on 1 January 2008 and partly in September 2008. It contains new rules relating to the obligation to disclose major shareholdings. This Act replaces the 'old' Act of 2 March 1989. The obligation to disclose major shareholdings is similar to that existing in other countries. The provisions of the Act of 2 May 2007 are mainly aimed at ensuring transposition of Directive 2004/109/EC of 15 December 2004 on the harmonization of transparency requirements in relation to information about issuers whose securities are admitted to trading on a regulated market and amending Directive 2001/34/EC. The main new features concern: (i) the notion of concerted exercise; (ii) the fact that the thresholds giving rise to disclosure may be passively exceeded, outside the context of an acquisition or a transfer of securities; and (iii) the combination of disclosures of shareholdings and control.

[465] The disclosure requirements are applicable to holdings in issuers having their registered office in Belgium and holdings in issuers having their registered office in a country that is not a member of the European Economic Area and that have chosen Belgium as Member State of origin in accordance with section 7(1) of the Act of 16 June 2006.

[466] As under the old law, the new act imposes on any person or entity, acting alone or jointly and exceeding a statutory holding threshold of 5% (or a lower threshold as may be provided under the articles of association of the issuer), the obligation of notifying same to the issuer and the FSMA. As previously, calculation of this threshold takes affiliated companies into account. It is therefore assessed on a consolidated basis in the hands of the holder of control. It also takes account of voting rights held by nominees.

The Notion of Concerted Exercise

[467] Section 3(1)(13°) of the Act of 2 May 2007 defines 'persons acting in concert'. These are:

- natural or legal persons who, in accordance with the Act of 1 April 2007 on public takeover bids, act in concert with the offeror, the offeree company or other persons on the basis of an agreement, whether express or tacit, verbal or written, with the aim of gaining control of the offeree company;
- natural or legal persons that have entered into an agreement for concerted exercise of their voting rights in order to conduct a lasting joint policy vis-à-vis the issuer concerned;
- natural or legal persons that have entered into an agreement relative to the possession, acquisition or transfer of voting securities.

[468] The notion of concerted exercise therefore presupposes an 'agreement' amongst parties, i.e., a contract and not a simple concerted practice. However, the FSMA considers that an agreement exists even if it is not binding. The difficulties of interpretation that the notion of concerted action can throw up are many.

'Passively' Exceeding Thresholds and Events Giving Rise to Disclosure without Acquisition or Transfer of Securities

[469] Under the old law, only the acquisition or transfer of voting securities triggered the obligation to notify a holding. The new rules also set down other situations, including passively exceeding thresholds, i.e., events altering the distribution of voting rights, or where the percentage of voting rights reaches, exceeds or falls below the thresholds laid down in section 6(1) of the Act of 2 May 2007. According to the legislative history to the act, such events include dilution following a capital increase not followed by a major shareholder, the retirement of shares by an issuer or where the lex societatis attributes multiple voting rights to one or more of the shareholders that have held their shares for a certain uninterrupted period or the exercise of options issued in favour of personnel in the form of a subscription right or the conversion of convertible bonds.

[470] If the exercise or non-exercise of financial instruments such as options, future options and other derivatives as well as certificates representative of unlisted shares results in a threshold being exceeded, the declarants must take account of this in their disclosures. In addition, if equivalent instruments are exercised or if they are not exercised but there is no resultant drop below a threshold, the holder must update its previous notification on 31 December of each year.

[471] Finally, signature, amendment or termination of a joint action agreement from which it follows that the voting percentages affected by the agreement or the percentage of one of the parties to the agreement attains or exceeds a threshold, whether upward or downward, triggers notification, even if there has not been any acquisition or transfer. When a joint action agreement is amended, a notification will also be required if the nature of the agreement is altered, even if the number of shares in question is not affected.

Disclosure Obligations Relating to the Notion of Control

[472] Under section 6(5) of the Act of 2 May 2007, any natural or legal person is deemed to acquire, transfer or indirectly hold voting shares of an issuer where either voting shares are acquired, transferred or held by an undertaking controlled by that natural or legal person or where it acquires or transfers control of an undertaking holding voting shares of an issuer. Hence, both holding and acquisition or transfer of control of an undertaking holding voting shares are covered by the act and collated under the idea of holding, acquisition or indirect transfer. Each of these situations must now be notified in a transparency disclosure.

[473] Finally, section 15, first paragraph, of the royal decree implementing the act requires declarants to disclose 'the chain of controlled undertakings through which the holding is effectively held'. It should be pointed out that joint control will furthermore fall within the definition of parties acting in concert as referred to in section 3(1)(13°)(b) of the Act of 2 May 2007 and must also be notified on this count.

Overview of the Rules relative to the New Transparency Regime

Scope of Application

[474] The Act of 2 May 2007 applies to issuers having issued shares admitted to trading on a regulated market or a MTF. An issuer is defined as being '*any legal person or person under private law or public law whose shares are admitted to trading on a regulated market*'. Additionally, the act states that an issuer whose shares are represented by listed certificates, even if they are issued by a third party, is to be equated to an issuer whose shares are listed.

[475] Under section 5 of the Act of 2 May 2007, the Act applies to: (i) issuers having their registered office in Belgium; and (ii) issuers whose registered office is established in a country that is not a member of the Economic European Area (EEA) and have chosen Belgium as Member State of origin in accordance with section 7(1) of the Act of 16 June 2006. Under the Directive 2004/109/EC of 15 December 2004, issuers established in a Member State are subject to the domestic law of said Member State. However, pursuant to section 20 of the Act of 2 May 2007, certain provisions of the act relating to language rules also apply to issuers of shares established in a Member State other than Belgium but whose shares are admitted to trading on a Belgian regulated market.

Voting Rights to Be Taken into Account in the Disclosure

[476] Just as under the old rules, the voting power of a declarant within an issuer is determined according to the voting shares or any equivalent securities that the declarant may hold. The following rules must therefore be taken into account:

- shares and other securities conferring voting rights: once a company has a class of shares admitted to listing, all the securities conferring voting rights, even unlisted shares, have to be disclosed. In this respect, profit-sharing certificates are taken into account according to the provisions of the articles of association of this issuer. As for non-voting shares, the declarant must, if appropriate, state the number of non-voting shares that he holds, even if they are not included in calculating proportions of voting rights;

- voting rights detached from share ownership: what are concerned here are thus voting rights held by a natural or legal person by virtue of an agreement providing for a temporary transfer of voting rights in return for consideration, a security or a pledger over securities conferring voting rights under the condition that the holder of the pledge (the pledger) controls the voting rights, a life tenancy over the voting securities on condition that the life tenant should control the voting rights, a securities deposit conferring the voting rights on condition that, in the absence of specific instructions from the holders of the securities, the depositary can exercise the voting rights as he sees fit, or a power of attorney under the condition that, in the absence of specific instructions from the holders of the securities, the attorney in fact may exercise the voting rights as he sees fit;
- equivalent financial instruments: under the provisions of the transparency directive, the Belgian legislation has only taken account of potential voting rights flowing from securities already issued. The royal decree implementing the Act of 2 May 2007 provides that, where shares and option contracts, future contracts, exchange contracts, interest rate futures contracts and any other derivative contracts confer rights on their holder, solely at his own initiative, to acquire securities conferring the already issued voting right to which they relate, said rights are equated to voting securities. Certificates representative of shares not admitted to trading on a regulated market are equated to voting securities where they give their holder the right to acquire, at his own initiative, already issued voting securities to which they relate. These certificates must be exchangeable unconditionally.

Calculation of Proportions

[477] In regard to calculation of the numerator, account is taken of all voting rights attaching to the securities in question, regardless of whether they might be suspended, resulting for example from the issuer holding its own shares (section 622, Companies Code). To this must be added both voting securities and voting rights attaching to equivalent securities, as well as voting rights held in isolation, such as by a life tenant or a pledgee creditor. Then there must be added in the hands of the natural or legal person holding control any holdings held by undertakings controlled by that person. Likewise, a principal, nominee or trustee must disclose securities held on his behalf by a third party. These securities are added to any securities that might be held in his own name. Finally, the act provides that persons acting in concert should add all the voting rights covered by their agreement.

[478] As regards the denominator, only the voting rights attaching to securities already issued by the issuer in question are taken into account.

[479] Finally, regarding potential voting rights not yet issued and non-voting shares, the law requires both the declarant and the issuer to report in each of the disclosures incumbent upon them the as yet unissued securities conferring voting rights. This essentially concerns warrants and convertible bonds. These will not, however, be included in the calculation of proportions. As for non-voting shares, these must also be mentioned by way of supplementary information.

Events Giving Rise to Notification

[480] The following events give rise to notification:

- the direct or indirect acquisition of voting securities if, as a result of this acquisition, the holder attains or exceeds, upward or downward, the statutory threshold of 5%, any multiple thereof or any lower or intermediary threshold as may be stated in the articles of association of the issuer;
- admission of the shares of an issuer to a regulated market for the first time in so far as either the statutory threshold or the threshold stated in the articles of association of the issuer is reached or exceeded;
- alteration of the distribution of voting rights where the percentage of voting rights exceeds a threshold upwards or downwards. The same applies to situations in which equivalent financial instruments are exercised or not exercised that do not give rise to a threshold being exceeded but nonetheless require the declarant to amend his previous notification;
- signature, amendment or assignment of a concert agreement where any of these events gives rise to a threshold being exceeded either by a party individually or by the concerted parties regarded as a whole. Amendment of the agreement must also be notified, even if the securities covered by the concert arrangement are not thereby affected;
- situations where the voting rights are separated from the securities to which they attach (cf. above) once a threshold is reached or exceeded by the transferor or transferee of the voting rights.

[481] Under section 10(1) of the Act of 2 May 2007, the notification obligation does not apply to voting securities acquired for the sole purposes of the netting and settlement of deals taking place within the three trading days following the transaction in question, or within the usual short-term settlement cycle.

Persons Required to Make Notification

[482] The persons required to make disclosures to the FSMA are various. They include the following:

- undertakings that hold control of the issuer and controlled undertakings. If control is exercised in cascade fashion, the obligation to take account of securities held indirectly does not apply at each stage in the chain, and the person (natural or legal) holding ultimate control is under an obligation to accumulate the voting rights held by all the undertakings under his or its control. In order to avoid a multiplicity of notifications, the act exempts controlled undertakings from having to make a notification required by the act if it is made by its parent company or, if the parent company is itself controlled by another entity, by its parent company. It is therefore possible to make just one disclosure, which is made by the undertaking exercising ultimate control;

- in the context of concert arrangements: the parties whose shares held under the arrangement exceed or reach a threshold must now make one single joint notification. It is permissible for natural persons acting in concert to maintain their anonymity vis-à-vis the issuer (but not the FSMA) provided: (i) their individual holding (not including the holdings of the other parties acting in concert) is less than the statutory threshold of 5% or a lower threshold as may be provided under the articles of association of the issuers; and (ii) their 'interest' in the issuer does not exceed 3%. In principle, parties acting in concert are under an obligation to disclose the figures relating to them personally over and above the holding held under the concert arrangement. However, natural persons that separately hold less than 1% can just disclose the overall holding they hold in concert, both to the issuer and to the FSMA. By contrast, if there is only one natural person in the concert arrangement or if only one natural person in the concert holds less than 1%, the holding of said natural person may not be aggregated and will therefore continue to be reported separately in the disclosure;
- where voting rights are separated from the securities to which they attach: in principle, in the case of a 'transfer' of voting rights independent from ownership of the securities to which they relate, the transferor must make a notification to the extent it exceeds a threshold. The acquirer of the voting rights is also required to notify his holding if it reaches or exceeds a threshold. Where such situations change or are terminated with the result that a threshold is reached or exceeded, new notifications have to be made. The same applies in the case of transfers of voting rights in the context of a life tenancy, provided the life tenant controls the voting rights. In the case of a deposit, the depositary is only required to make a notification if it has power, failing specific instructions from the holder of the securities, to exercise the voting rights as it sees fit. In the case of a power of attorney, the holder of the securities conferring the voting rights may merely make a single notification provided he clearly explains what the situation resulting from the transaction will be in terms of voting rights when the powers are terminated;
- in the case of third parties acting as nominees: this essentially covers the cases of agency, carrying agreements and fiduciary or trust arrangements. In this respect, it will be necessary to examine who it is that has control over the voting rights;
- issuers with a holding: the act expressly requires an issuer that acquires, disposes of or holds its own securities to make a notification in the cases set down in the act. In this regard, no account is taken of the fact that the voting rights might be suspended pursuant to section 622 of the Companies Code.

[483] Finally, the new transparency act increases the burden of obligations incumbent on issuers. They must disclose a series of types of information concerning the denominator and any thresholds provided for in the articles of association. They must also disclose all notifications they receive within a period of three trading days following receipt, which contrasts with previous practice.

TAKEOVER BIDS

[484] Directive 2004/25/EC of 21 April 2004 on takeover bids (the 'Takeovers Directive') has just be transposed into Belgian law by the Act of 1 April 2007 (the 'Takeover Bid') and its two implementing royal decrees of 27 April 2007. Apart from transposing the directive, the Takeover Bids Act is more broadly aimed at modernizing the rules governing takeover bids and therefore includes most of the provisions concerning bid procedures that were hitherto contained in Chapter II of the Act of 2 March 1989 and the Royal Decree of 8 November 1989 on takeover bids and changes in corporate control.

Scope of Application

[485] The scope of application of the Takeover Bids Act is defined in its section 4. That section states that the act covers the following categories of bids.

A Voluntary Offer of a Public Nature Made in Belgium

[486] The Takeover Bids Act draws no distinction as to nature of the offeree company or the nature of the securities subject to the bid.

[487] The Takeover Bids Act defines the notion of 'public nature' by, at least essentially, incorporating the criteria set down in the Royal Decree of 7 July 1999 on the public nature of financial operations. These criteria for determining the public nature of a bid have nonetheless been amended to bring them into line with those contained in the Act of 16 June 2006 on public offers of investment instruments and the admission of investment instruments to trading on regulated markets (as amended by the Act of 17 July 2013).

[488] Thus, a voluntary takeover bid will be public in nature where:

- –a communication containing sufficient information on the conditions of the bid to enable a holder of securities to decide whether to transfer his securities and to embark on a publicity procedure is distributed in Belgium; or
- –a publicity procedure is embarked on with the intention of announcing or recommending the acquisition offer.

[489] In the same terms as are contained in the Act of 16 June 2006, the Takeover Bids Act sets forth certain categories of bids that are not public in nature:

- bids made in Belgium that concern securities that are only distributed amongst qualified investors within the meaning of section 10 of the Act of 16 June 2006;
- bids made under identical terms in Belgium to less than 150 natural or legal persons other than qualified investors within the meaning of section 10 of the Act of 16 June 2006;
- bids in respect of securities whose unitary par value amounts to at least EUR100 000.

[490] However, this exception does not apply in the case of a compulsory public offer as defined.

A Mandatory Bid Launched Over Securities Issued by a Company Having its Registered Office in Belgium and Admitted to Trading on a Regulated Market or an Officially Recognised Organised Market

[491] The Takeover Bids Act reduces the scope of application of mandatory bids to companies whose securities are admitted to trading on an organized market designated by royal decree, thus catering for the difficulties that faced the FSMA under the Act of 2 March 1989 which applies to all companies having made a public invitation to invest, including companies whose shares are held by more than fifty shareholders. In the context of its oversight of mandatory offers relating to securities of unlisted companies, the FSMA was to a large extent dependent on the opinions brought before it by the parties concerned since transparency disclosures did not apply to this type of company. Furthermore, mention of a company on the list of companies having made public invitation to invest referred to in section 438, fourth paragraph, of the Companies Code was purely declaratory in nature, it thus offered no legal security as to the status of the company in question.

A Mandatory Bid Launched Over the Securities of a Company Having its Registered Office in Another Member State of the EEA, Whose Principal Market Is Situated in Belgium and Whose Securities Are Not Admitted to Trading on a Regulated Market in the Member State in Which It Has Its Registered Office

[492] This type of bid is nonetheless only subject to the Takeovers Bid Act as regards the aspects relative to recognition of a prospectus approved in another Member State, promotional communications distributed in Belgium, the consideration offered and the bid procedure.

[493] Since enactment of the new rules, mandatory bids relating to the securities of a company having its registered office in another Member State and whose securities are not traded on a regulated market in said Member State but whose principal market is situated in Belgium are thus subject to Belgian law as regards issues relating to the prospectus and promotional communications, in relation to which the FSMA is required to exercise its control powers.

A Mandatory Bid Launched in Belgium Over Voting Securities Not Covered under §§496 to 498 Above

[494] For this type of bid, only the rules relative to information apply.

Squeeze-Out Launched Pursuant to Section 513(1) of the Companies Code

[495] This type of bid is discussed in further detail in the next chapter.

Voluntary Takeover Bids

Conditions for Being Admissible

[496] The Royal Decree of 27 April 2007 on takeover bids sets out the conditions for a bid to be admissible and, apart from a few exceptions, restates most of the provisions of the Royal Decree of 8 November 1989 applying in this domain.

[497] To be admissible, a takeover bid must meet the following requirements:

- the bid must cover all the securities conferring or granting access to voting rights;
- in the case of a takeover bid, the funds necessary to consummate the bid must be available either in an account held with a credit institution or in the form of an irrevocable unconditional credit granted to the offeror by a credit institution;
- in the case of a tender bid, the offeror must have either securities to offer in exchange or power to issue them or the right to acquire them in sufficient quantities and within the time provided for payment and, if it does not have power to issue them, it must at least be able de facto or *de iure* to procure that the legal person concerned shale issue the securities;
- the bid, and its terms and conditions, must comply with the Royal Decree of 27 April 2007; additionally, the terms of the bid must be such, especially as regards the price, that they should normally enable the offeror to obtain the desired result;
- the offeror must undertake that, as far as matters within its control are concerned, it will carry the bid through to its conclusion;
- receipt of acceptances and payment of the price are assured by a credit institution or a stock-broking firm.

[498] The Royal Decree of 27 April 2007 on takeover bids also sets down two new rules, as follows:

- if the bid is to relate to securities of different classes, the prices offered for each such class may not bear any differences other than such as follow from the respective characteristics of each class;
- anyone who fails, at the request of and within the time set down by the FSMA to file a notice confirming its intention of launching a bid in a reasonable

period and anyone acting in concert therewith may not make a bid over the securities of the offeree company in question for a period of six months as from publication of the said notice or expiry of the time allowed by the FSMA, unless they evidence to it that the circumstances, the situation of the offeree company or the shareholders of the persons concerned have changed significantly.

Announcement of a Takeover Bid

[499] The royal decree also confirms application of the existing rules as regards announcement of the bid. Thus whoever proposes making a takeover bid must first lodge a notice together with a bid file comprising a draft prospectus and promotional notices with the FSMA.

Takeover Bid Price

[500] As previously provided for by the Royal Decree of 8 November 1989, the price must be such as it allows the offeror to obtain the desired result. How the price is fixed is a matter for the offeror alone, and the FSMA may not interfere directly in that decision.

[501] Hence, in a voluntary takeover bid, the FSMA has no authority to judge whether the price fixed by the offeror is equitable and therefore cannot refuse to approve a bid on the ground that the price is inadequate. However, the question could be trickier in the case of a bid launched by a controlling shareholder, since a takeover bid made in that context offers fairly weak conditions of competitiveness, that are unable to correct any insufficiency in the price. Moreover, because the majority of the board of directors of the offeree company are representatives of the offeror and they are not bound to abstain (Tractebel judgment of 19 January 2004), the independence of the notice issued by the board of directors in such circumstances will be compromised. Finally, because the offeror controls the offeree company, it is free to choose when it will launch its offer, which it is likely to do when the share price is depressed.

[502] In such circumstances, some maintain that the FSMA has power to verify the price. Its power to do so was said to be founded in section 15 of the Royal Decree of 8 November 1989 in that it enabled the FSMA to act in the interests of the holders of securities, and in section 3(4°) in so far as it imposes certain restrictions in relation to the price. In its 1999-2000 report, however, the Commission refused to endorse this construction, saying that the price must be subject solely to the will of the offeror. Section 16(1) of the Act of 2 March 1989, amended by the Act of 2 August 2002, would incidentally seem to support the FSMA's view to the extent that it limits the Commission's powers just to oversight of the royal decrees, to the exclusion of the general principles set forth in the act. The FSMA's sole power thus lies in its ability to refuse to approve the prospectus.

[503] Nonetheless, where a takeover bid was launched by the controlling shareholder of the offeree company, the FSMA would usually ask the offeror to have a fairness opinion prepared by an independent expert. The independence of the expert, of great importance in this respect, could be assessed in light of the notion of independent expert under the CBFA's circular D2/F/2000/5. Thus, when Suez, a French public limited liability company, made a bid over the Electrabel shares not yet in its possession, four fairness opinions were issued by three international banks and one Belgian bank. The institutions that supplied the opinions requested by the offeror had themselves to prove their independence in relation to the operation whilst it fell to the board of directors of the offeree company that requested the other two opinions to judge the independence of the other two institutions concerned.

[504] It is with such situations in mind that the Royal Decree of 27 April 2007 on takeover bids states that, where a takeover bid is launched over the voting shares of a Belgian company by a offeror that, at the time when it notified its intention of launching the offer, exercised control over the company in question (within the meaning of section 5 of the Companies Code), the independent directors (within the meaning of section 524 of the Companies Code) of the offeree company have an obligation to appoint one or more independent experts (within the meaning of section 22 of the Royal Decree of 27 April 2007) with the task of preparing a report in which they value the offeree company.

[505] If the offeree company does not have independent directors, its board appoints the expert or experts with the approval of the FSMA.

[506] The same royal decree makes a second qualification to the principle that the FSMA may not directly interfere in how the price is set. Apart from the obligation on a offeror that has given an undertaking before closure of the bid to acquire the company's shares at a price greater than the bid to reopen its bid at that price and pay the price difference to those that have responded to the bid, it is now no longer permitted for it or any persons acting in concert with it for a period of one year as from the end of the bid period to acquire securities that were covered by the takeover bid under terms that are more advantageous than provided for in the takeover bid in question, unless the difference in price is paid to all holders of shares that responded to the bid.

Obligations on the Parties to the Bid

[507] Publication of the takeover bid notice triggers a number of obligations on the part of the parties to the bid.

[508] Thus, section 10 of the Royal Decree of 27 April 2007 confirms the bid parties' obligation to refrain from publishing or procuring the publication of statements, communications or documents containing information that is false or liable to mislead the public in direct or indirect relation to a bid, counter-bid or over-bid.

[509] In addition, the Royal Decree of 27 April 2007 confirms the obligation of reporting to the FSMA all operations carried out on securities of the offeree company by the offeror or companies whose securities are offered as consideration, although a number of details are added regarding application of this principle:

- reporting to the FSMA must be made on the date of the operation in question or the next working day;

- reporting extends to loans of stocks or the unwinding prior to term of stock loans relating to securities carrying or conferring access to voting rights in the offeree company, the offeror or the company whose securities are offered as consideration;
- the reporting obligation applies to persons that directly or indirectly hold at least 1% of the voting securities of the offeror or offeree company;
- the FSMA publicizes these reports daily on its web site.

Drafting, Approval and Distribution of the Prospectus

[510] Takeover bids do not constitute public bids within the meaning of the Act of 16 June 2006 on takeover bids of investment instruments or Directive 2003/71/EC of 4 November 2003. Takeover bids are therefore exclusively governed by the Takeover Bids Act.

[511] This act confirms the principle that a prospectus must be drafted in the case of a takeover bid, and adds a number of important details.

[512] First, in order to ensure that the prospectus is clear and visible, the Takeover Bids Act lays down the obligation of drafting a prospectus summary briefly setting out in non-technical language the principal features of the bid, a description of the offeror and the offeree company, the offeror's intentions and, in the case of a tender offer, details relating to the securities offered in exchange as well as 7% and the issuer of said securities.

[513] In addition, the prospectus must now be drafted in accordance with certain rules.

[514] Under the language rules applying to the prospectus, it has to be prepared in French and Dutch unless the offeror shows that the offeree company habitually publishes its financial information in just one national language or in a language customary in the international financial world. In that case, the FSMA can agree to the prospectus being written in that single national language or in another language. In any event, the prospectus summary is written in or translated into French and Dutch.

[515] The only decisions the FSMA can take are those set forth in the relevant legislation, i.e., approval of the prospectus, rejection of the prospectus, a total dispensation with the requirement for a prospectus or a finding that the dossier submitted to it is incomplete. In this case, the FSMA must state what items are missing from the dossier.

[516] Finally, the act provides that the offeror may request recognition of the prospectus relating to the bid if it has previously been approved by the competent authority in another Member State under Article 4 of Directive 2004/25/EC.

Drafting, Approval and Distribution of the Reply Memorial

[517] The board of directors of the offeree company is required to submit a reply memorial for approval by the FSMA within five working days following intimation by the FSMA of the duly approved prospectus.

[518] The reply memorial must be reasoned and set forth:

- the effects of implementation of the bid on the entire interests of the company, holders of securities, creditors and workforce, including jobs;
- the view of the board regarding the offeror's strategic plans for the offeree company and their probable effects on the activities of the company, its financial performances and on jobs;
- the view of the board regarding the opportunity for the shareholders to transfer their titles.

[519] If the members of the board cannot reach a unanimous opinion, the opinions of the different directors will be mentioned, with indication of which directors are independent.

[520] It should be noted that the board of directors will also be involved at a previous stage in the process of preparing the prospectus, since the act provides that, if the board takes the view that the draft prospectus sent to it by the FSMA contains lacunae or information liable to mislead holders of securities in the offeree company, it must inform the FSMA and the offeror thereof no later than five working days following receipt of the draft prospectus.

Period for Acceptance of the Bid and Closure Thereof

[521] The period for accepting the bid may be neither less than two weeks, in order to ensure that holders of securities are properly informed, nor greater than ten weeks.

[522] Section 31 of the Royal Decree of 27 April 2007 on takeover bids provides for two cases in which the period for acceptance of the bid is extended. The first is where a general meeting of the offeree company is called to deliberate on the bid and, in particular, on action liable to frustrate the bid. The second relates to the acquisition by the offeror or a person acting in concert with him (or any undertaking to that effect), during the bid period but outside the context of the bid, of securities to which the bid relates at a price greater than that under the bid. Extension of the bid benefits the holders of securities that have not yet accepted the bid. Holders of securities that have already accepted the bid automatically benefit from the increase in the price.

Sell-Out Procedure

[523] Section 44 of the Royal Decree of 27 April 2007 on takeover bids introduces into Belgian law the sell-out procedure applying to public companies.

[524] Thus, since 1 September 2007, an offeror that, following a public offer or the reopening thereof, possesses 95% of the capital carrying voting rights, 95% of the voting securities and 90% of the voting capital forming the subject matter of the bid, can be forced by any holder of securities to buy his securities carrying voting rights or conferring access to voting rights at the bid price.

[525] For the purposes of calculating the thresholds set out above, the royal decree states that account has to be taken of the securities held by persons acting in concert with the offeror within the meaning of section 513(1), fourth paragraph, of the Companies Code.

[526] The holders of the securities must send their sell-out application to the offeror by recorded delivery letter with confirmation of receipt within three months following expiry of the period for acceptance of the bid. Furthermore, the offeror must notify the FSMA of such applications.

Defences Against a Hostile Bid

[527] The Takeovers Directive states the principle of 'neutrality', in terms of which the board of a company informed that a takeover bid has been launched may not enact measures likely to frustrate the bid. However, the Directive does say that the Member States may provide that these rules do not apply to companies whose registered office is located within their territory. Member States making use of this option must nevertheless offer companies established within their territory the possibility of applying the neutrality rules under their articles of association.

[528] In Belgium, the Takeover Bids Act provides that, unless the articles of association provide otherwise, the neutrality rule is not binding on companies having their registered office in Belgium and so allows the board of a company informed of the launch of a takeover bid to take such measures likely to frustrate the bid as are permitted under the Companies Code.

[529] Moreover, the act provides that the FSMA has express powers to ensure that such measures are due and proper. As a corollary to this obligation, the target company will for its part be subject to a duty of information vis-à-vis the FSMA. Thus, by contrast with the previous state of affairs, the FSMA's regulatory powers are not limited to the specific takeovers legislation but extend to the provisions of the Companies Code relative to anti-takeover defence measures.

[530] Section 46 of the Takeover Bids Act nonetheless provides that the articles of association of a company having its registered office in Belgium and at least part of whose voting securities are admitted to trading on a regulated market may provide for application of the rules of passivity and neutrality which imply that the board of directors shall not take any measures likely to frustrate the bid unless said measures have been duly authorized by a resolution adopted by the general meeting of shareholders. Introduction of such a clause into the articles of association said decisions must be notified to the FSMA by the company's general meeting of shareholders.

Mandatory Bids

[531] Under the old rules, an acquisition of voting securities – or of equivalent securities – triggered an obligation to launch a bid if the acquirer had control of the company in question and paid an additional price.

[532] However, these old rules provided for an exception to this principle, in that an acquisition of securities to be subscribed for pursuant to a capital increase did not trigger the obligation to launch a bid. It was nonetheless generally accepted that certain transactions, like mergers, did not require a bid to be launched.

[533] Just as under the old legislation, the Takeovers Directive aims to protect minority shareholders where, further to an acquisition of securities carried out by a person or by several persons acting in concert, said person or persons should hold control of a company whose securities are admitted to trading on a regulated market. In such a case, the acquirer is required to launch a bid addressed to all holders of voting securities; the bid must cover all of their securities and be issued at a fair price. However, the Takeovers Directive does not stipulate what percentage of voting securities will constitute control of a company but does contain details as regards the 'fair price' and the nature of the consideration offered by the offeror, especially if that consideration comprises securities.

[534] Taking particular account of the percentages that have been fixed in the countries neighbouring Belgium, the threshold enacted in the new Takeover Bids Act is 30%. Hence, section 5 of the new act provides that:

> Where, pursuant to an acquisition made by a person, by persons acting in concert with him or persons acting on behalf of such persons, a person directly or indirectly holds more than 30% of the voting securities of a company having its registered office in Belgium and at least part of whose voting securities are admitted to trading on a regulated market or on a multilateral trading facility designated by the King, he is obliged, under such terms as are fixed by the King, to launch a takeover bid over the entire securities carrying voting rights or conferring access to voting rights that have been issued by that company. He shall notify the FSMA hereof.
>
> For the purposes of the immediately preceding paragraph, the King may, by order deliberated in Cabinet and enacted on the recommendation of the FSMA, fix another percentage or an additional percentage of voting securities in order to take account of developments in the financial markets and, as appropriate, enact transitional measures.

Offeree Companies

[535] Section 5 of the Takeover Bids Act therefore covers 'companies having their registered office in Belgium and at least part of whose voting securities are admitted to trading on a regulated market or on a multilateral trading facility designated by the King'.

[536] The Takeover Bids Act also provides that the mandatory takeover bid rules apply to offeree companies having their registered office in another Member State but whose principal market is situated in Belgium, but only as regards matters relative to the consideration offered and the bid procedure (section 4(1)(3°), Takeover Bids Act).

Securities Covered

[537] In order to align with the transparency rules, this threshold has been fixed on the basis of securities carrying voting rights, whether or not they represent the share capital (but disregarding securities carrying potential voting rights). However, the bid must relate not only to the voting securities but also to securities potentially conferring voting rights, since holders of such securities also feel the effects of the change in control of the offeree company. Incidentally, this approach is in line with the current regulations.

[538] It should equally be pointed out that indirect holdings now also have to be taken into account in calculating the threshold.

Powers of the FSMA and the Courts

[539] The Takeover Bids Act does not substantially alter the regulatory powers of the FSMA and of the Brussels Court of Appeal as regards takeovers, but does make some slight refinements.

The FSMA's Regulatory Powers

[540] The FSMA is invested with power to oversee application of the takeovers legislation. Nonetheless, under section 35(1) of the Takeover Bids Act, this power is no longer limited, as it previously was, just to the royal decrees but is extended to the Takeover Bids Act itself. Similarly, the FSMA's power to grant exceptions to the takeover rules in certain cases has also been extended to the Takeover Bids Act.

[541] In the context of this oversight, the FSMA has power to '*enact* necessary *measures and issue instructions to ensure correct application of the provisions of Part II of this act and its implementing decrees*', whereby each order or prohibition may carry a financial penalty. Here again, the FSMA's powers are extended to the act itself. These measures and orders are set out in section 36(1) of the Takeover Bids Act and particularly include the powers:

- to prohibit or suspend the bid;
- to order the launch of a mandatory bid;
- to order, prohibit, suspend or require withdrawal of the distribution of communications of a promotional nature; and
- order the target company to publish the reply memorial.

[542] The FSMA may publish its orders and decisions. However, conscious of the deleterious effect of such publication, the statute proscribes any publicity that might risk 'seriously disrupting the financial markets or causing disproportionate harm to the parties in question'.

[543] Independently of its power to attach financial penalties for breach of some of its decisions, the FSMA may, as in the past, impose administrative fines and criminal penalties.

[544] In addition, the FSMA has certain powers of investigation. Section 36(1), second paragraph (3°), of the Takeover Bids Act enables the FSMA to 'require the parties to the bid or parties which the FSMA has reasonable cause to believe are obliged to launch a mandatory bid, together with persons that they control or that are controlled by them, to furnish information and documents to the *FSMA*', and the FSMA may also 'carry out site inspections and appraisals, take cognisance and copies on site of any document, file and entry and gain access to any IT system in order to satisfy itself of compliance with the provisions of Part II of this act and its implementing decrees, providing always that these powers of investigation shall not extend to private *dwellings*' (section 36(1), second paragraph (13°) of the Takeover Bids Act).

[545] Finally, section 8 of the Royal Decree of 27 April 2007 now provides that 'where a person, itself or via an intermediary, has made statements giving rise amongst the general public to questions as to its intention of launching a bid, the F*SMA* may require that person to publish a communiqué clarifying its intentions. The F*SMA* may grant a period not exceeding ten working days for publication of said communiqué'. If said person fails to comply, he may not make a bid for a period of six months unless he shows that the circumstances, the situation of the target company or the shareholders of the persons concerned have significantly changed.

Jurisdiction of Brussels Court of Appeal

[546] The Act of 2 August 2002 conferred jurisdiction on the Brussels Court of Appeal *for* all disputes relating to takeover bids, albeit making the president of Brussels Commercial Court solely competent to rule on ex parte petitions lodged in cases of absolute necessity.

[547] This competence, which used to figure in section 584 of the Judicial Code, has been abrogated by the Takeover Bids Act and the bulk of the *disputes* in relation to takeovers are now heard before the Brussels Court of Appeal. In addition, in respect of petitions lodged in cases of absolute necessity, section 41(6) of the Takeover Bids Act now provides that 'in cases of absolute necessity, an ex parte petition may be raised before Brussels Court of Appeal seeking interim measures until such time as it rules after a hearing of all parties'. The Court of Appeal therefore now has exclusive jurisdiction for all claims on the merits and interim claims relative to application of the Takeovers Act as well as any claim liable to have the effect of triggering the opening of a takeover bid or altering the conditions, procedural course or result of a takeover bid.

SQUEEZE-OUTS

Introduction

[548] Squeeze-outs are now governed by the Takeover Bids Act and the Royal Decree of 27 April 2007 on squeeze-outs. This decree to a large extent restates the previous regulatory framework applying to such operations. This regulatory framework, the basis provision of which is contained in section 513 of the Companies Code, was nonetheless amended in certain respects. Since 1 September 2007, the date when the Takeover Bids Act and the Royal Decree of 27 April 2007 on squeeze-outs came into force, section 513 of the Companies Code reads as follows:

Section 513(1). A natural or legal person, or two or more natural or legal persons acting in concert and holding jointly with the company 95% of the securities conferring voting rights of a public limited liability company that makes or has made public offers to investors, may, further to a squeeze-out bid, acquire the entire securities carrying voting rights or giving access to voting rights.

Upon completion of the procedure, the securities that shall not have been not presented, regardless of whether or not the owner has revealed himself, are deemed transferred ipso iure to that person upon consignment of the price. *[. . .]*

Following completion of the squeeze-out bid, the company shall no longer be regarded as having made or making public offers to investors unless bonds issued by that company are still held amongst the general public.

Persons acting in concert are deemed to be:

a) natural or legal persons acting in concert within the meaning of section 3(1)(5°)(a) of the Act of 1 April 2007 on takeover bids;

b) natural or legal persons that have entered into an agreement relative to exercise in concert of their voting rights with the aim of conducting a lasting policy in relation to the company concerned;

c) natural or legal persons that have entered into an agreement relative to the possession, acquisition or transfer of securities conferring voting rights.

(2). Any natural or legal person that, acting alone or in concert, holds 90% of the securities conferring voting rights in a public limited liability company that has not made or does not make public offers to investors may make a squeeze-out bid in relation to the entire securities conferring voting rights of that company.

Upon completion of the procedure, with the exception of securities whose owner has expressly intimated in writing that he refuses to dispose thereof, the securities that have not been presented are deemed transferred ipso iure to that person upon consignment of the price. Dematerialised securities whose owner has expressly intimated in writing that he refuses to dispose thereof are converted ipso iure into registered securities and are entered in the securities register through the offices of the board of directors.

[. . .]

The bid referred to in the first paragraph of this subsection is not subject to either Title II of Royal Decree no. 185 of 9 July 1935 on the regulation of banks and the rules governing issues of securities and stocks or Chapter II of the Act of 2 March 1989 on the publicity of major holdings in stock-market listed companies and governing takeover bids or section 4 of the Act of 4 December 1990 on financial transactions and financial markets.

(2/1) [. . .]

(3). The King may regulate squeeze-outs falling under subsection 2 and particularly determine the procedure to be followed and the terms for fixing the squeeze-out bid price. In this regard, he shall ensure that bearers of securities are duly informed and treated equally.

(4). The extract of the judicial decision that has become res iudicata or provisionally enforceable and ruling on the terms of a forced transfer is filed and published in accordance with section 75.

[549] Apart from squeeze-out bids, section 513 of the Companies Code thus also covers squeeze-outs applying to private companies by setting out separate rules for this type of company, which are explained below.

Squeeze-Out Bids

Offeree Companies

[550] Section 4 of the Takeover Bid Act provides that it applies to all squeeze-outs within the meaning of section 513(1) of the Companies Code. That provision is aimed at public limited liability companies and partnerships limited by shares that make or have made public offers to investors.

[551] In this regard, section 438 of the Companies Code states that a public limited liability company is regarded as making or having made public offers to investors where it makes a public call for savings in Belgium or abroad by means of a public subscription offer, a public sale offer, a public tender offer or an admission to listing, within the meaning of section 4 of the Companies Code, of bonds or securities, whether or not representative of the capital, whether or not conferring voting rights, as well as securities giving a right to subscription for or acquisition of such securities or conversion into such securities.

[552] On this score, under section 202 of the Royal Decree of 30 January 2001 implementing the Companies Code the public nature of an offer for subscription, sale or tender within the meaning of section 438, first paragraph, of the Companies Code that is made in Belgium is determined in accordance with the provisions of section 3 of the Act of 16 June 2006 on the public offer of financial instruments. The same decree nonetheless underlines the fact that an offer intended exclusively for the current or former shareholders of the company or of undertakings affiliated to it is not deemed to be public.

Securities Covered

[553] The new wording of section 513 of the Companies Code provides that the securities covered by the squeeze-out bid are securities carrying voting rights and securities giving access to voting rights, thus replacing the notion of securities conferring voting rights as contained in the older wording of section 513 of the Companies Code.

[554] Just as under the old rules, profit-sharing certificates that do not carry voting rights and non-voting shares are therefore not covered by these types of offers. However, the question is trickier if, at the end of a squeeze-out bid, it is only such securities that are still distributed amongst the general public. Section 513 of the Companies Code provides that, after completion of the squeeze-out, the company will no longer be regarded as making or having made public offers to investors unless bonds issued by that company are still distributed amongst the general public. The act says nothing in this regard but invests power in the King to determine the time from which the securities of a company are deemed no longer to be distributed amongst the general public.

95% Threshold

[555] As in the past, this concerns the threshold of 95% of the securities conferring voting rights.

[556] This figure is assessed on the basis of all of the securities covered by the squeeze-out bid, without it being necessary for the offeror to hold that percentage of each class of securities covered.

[557] Section 513 expressly provides that the securities held by the company have to be added to those held by the offeror.

Action in Concert

[558] The notion of action in concert is now defined in section 513 of the Companies Code itself. The definition contained in section 513 is more extensive than as applied under the old rules and now covers the following persons:

1. natural or legal persons acting in concert within the meaning of section 3(1)(5°)(a) of the Takeover Bids Act;
2. natural or legal persons that have entered into an agreement relating to the concerted exercise of their voting rights for the purpose of conducting a lasting joint policy *vis-à-vis* the company concerned;
3. natural or legal persons that have entered into an agreement relating to the possession, acquisition and transfer of securities conferring voting rights.

This third category is aimed at indirect holdings of the offeror, which are taken account of and added to the securities held by the offeror to establish the 95% threshold.

[559] Section 3 (1)(5°)(a) of the Takeover Bids Act defines persons acting in concert as natural or legal persons that cooperate with the offeror, the offeree company or other persons on the basis of an agreement, express or tacit, verbal or written, with the aim of obtaining control of the offeree company, frustrating a bid or maintaining control of the offeree company.

[560] In this regard, the Takeover Bids Act goes on to state that, for the purposes of section 3(1)(5°), natural or legal persons that are related within the meaning of section 11 of the Companies Code to other natural or legal persons are deemed to be persons acting in concert with those other persons and *inter se*;

[561] As in the past, a squeeze-out bid cannot be launched at a company's initiative over its own securities. The CBFA had occasion to restate this in the context of the buy-out bid launched by Concentra. The company wanted to launch a squeeze-out bid over the remainder of its own shares, arguing that it was acting in concert with the majority shareholder. However, the CBFA cited the history to the legislation that was previously applicable in taking the view that this procedure, which had been embarked upon merely in favour of the controlling shareholders, could not be initiated by the company itself, since the interests of these shareholders necessarily could not be confused with those of the company.

Requirements Concerning the Bid

[562] The requirements specific to squeeze-out bids, which are to a large degree the same as those under the Royal Decree of 8 November 1989, which used to apply in this field, are as follows:

(a) the squeeze-out bid must relate to the entire securities carrying voting rights or giving access to voting rights issued by the offeree company and not yet held by the offeror, persons acting in concert with the offeror within the meaning of section 513(1), fourth paragraph, of the Companies Code and the offeree company itself;

(b) the offeror, persons acting in concert with the offeror and the offeree company itself must hold 95% of the voting securities of the offeree company, which makes or has made public offers to investors within the meaning of section 438 of the Companies Code;

   the price must comprise a sum of money and therefore may not be represented by securities issued by the offeror. The funds necessary for consummating the bid have to be available either in an account with a credit institution or in the form of an irrevocable, unconditional credit accorded to the offeror by a credit institution; the funds are frozen to ensure payment of the purchase price for the securities acquired under the bid or are allocated exclusively for that purpose;

(c) the bid, as well as its terms and conditions, must be in conformity with the provisions of the Royal Decree of 27 April 2007 on squeeze-outs. These terms and conditions must be such as to safeguard the interests of the holders of securities;

(d) if the bid relates to securities of different classes, the prices offered for each such class may not bear any differences other than as result from the respective characteristics of each class;

(e) the offeror undertakes, in so far as is within his power, to bring the bid to its conclusion, although this requirement is not to be construed as meaning that the operation is irrevocable;

(f) receipt of acceptances and payment of the price has to be carried out by a credit institution or a stock-broking firm.

The Squeeze-Out Price

[563] The Royal Decree of 27 April 2007 on squeeze-outs merely restates the principle that the price must be of such a nature as to safeguard the interests of the bearers of securities without providing the offeror with a formula enabling him to determine the price applicable to the bid.

[564] It nevertheless seems that the offeror must use a generally accepted, commonly applied valuation method to set the price. In addition, the intervention of an independent expert will give an objective quality to the price proposed by the offeror.

Procedure

(1) Notice

[565] Any company wanting to launch a squeeze-out must advise the FSMA beforehand.

[566] This notice must contain particulars that show that the requirements set out above have been met. The notice must particularly state the price and the main terms of the bid. In addition, the notice is accompanied by a dossier containing the draft prospectus and a report by an expert, both prepared in accordance with the Royal Decree of 27 April 2007 on squeeze-outs.

[567] The FSMA makes this notice public no later than the working day following receipt of it. The charges for this publication are paid by the offeror, and it states where members of the public can obtain the report of the expert attached to the notice free of charge. Under current FSMA practice, the notice announcing the bid is notified to a press agency and placed on the FSMA's web site on the day of receipt or the next day. It is also published as quickly as possible in two newspapers.

(2) Designation of an Independent Expert

[568] The expert is designated by the offeror, and his appointment need not be approved by the FSMA, which merely assesses the expert's independence in terms of the criteria set forth in the Royal Decree of 27 April 2007 on squeeze-outs.

[569] In this regard, the royal decree considers that the following persons may not act as the independent expert:

- the statutory auditor or chartered accountant of the offeror, the offeree company or companies affiliated to them;
- any person with which the statutory auditor or chartered accountant of the offeror, the offeree company or companies affiliated to them has a link within the meaning of section 133(4) of the Companies Code;
- any person who is paid by the offeror, the offeree company or companies affiliated to them for any other engagement in connection with the proposed squeeze-out.

[570] The royal decree goes on to set forth a series of circumstances that are presumed to give rise to a situation of dependence or a conflict of interests:

- the existence of a legal or capital-holding connection between the expert and the offeror or the offeree company, companies affiliated to them or their advisers;
- the existence on the expert's part of a pecuniary interest in the success of the squeeze-out, other than such as results from his engagement;
- where, during the two years preceding filing of the bid notice, any other engagement has been carried out on behalf of the offeror, the offeree company or companies affiliated to them;
- the existence on the expert's part of a debt due to or by the offeror, the offeree company or companies affiliated to them in so far as this debt is such as might create a relationship of economic dependence.

(4) The Expert's Report

[571] The report drawn up by the independent expert must contain at least the following elements:

- a description of the identity of the offeree company, the structure and spread of its shareholder structure, the entire undertakings to which it belongs, the businesses carried on by it and their spread, its recent developments and the identities of its officers;
- the latest annual accounts of the offeree company and the reports pertaining thereto or, if they are available, its latest consolidated accounts and the reports pertaining thereto, together with a more recent statement of changes if important changes have occurred since the balance sheet date of those accounts or if they date back more than nine months;
- a precise description of the various securities to which the bid relates.

[572] In addition, this report now also has to contain:

- a valuation, supported by detailed figures of the securities covered by the bid, using relevant methods in light of the nature and business of the company concerned and based on appropriate facts and suppositions;
- an indication of the valuation methods applied by the expert, the elements of fact and suppositions he has taken as a basis, the sources he has used and the result he has arrived at by means of the valuation methods used;
- an analysis of the valuation work carried out by the offeror;
- the expert's opinion on whether or not the price offered safeguards the interests of the holders of securities;
- adequate justification of the expert's independence vis-à-vis the offeror, the offeree company and the companies affiliated to them;
- the fee received by the expert, and an indication of the resources he has utilized in terms of staff and time, a description of the procedures he has carried out and mention of the persons he has contacted.

(5) Obligations During the Bid Period

[573] As in the past, the parties to the bid must refrain throughout the entire bid period from publishing or procuring the publication of statements, communications or documents containing information that is false or likely to mislead the public and relating directly or indirectly to the bid.

[574] Moreover, as from submission of the notice, the offeror and persons acting in concert with the offeror must refrain from acquiring securities falling under the bid under more favourable conditions than attach to the bid unless the offeror confers the benefit thereof to all parties to whom the bid is addressed.

(6) Possibility for Holders of Securities to Complain

[575] Holders of securities subject to the bid have a period of fifteen working days from publication of the notice and the independent expert's report to inform the FSMA of complaints they wish to make against the bid and, in particular, against the valuation of the securities of the offeree company or the price offered, having regard to the safeguarding of their interests.

[576] At the end of this fifteen working day period, the FSMA may notify the offeror of remarks it has to make on the bid. These remarks are notified to the offeror, the offeree company, the market maker concerned if the securities of the offeree company are admitted to trading on a Belgian regulated market and to any holders of securities that have intimated their complaints to the FSMA. The FSMA can make its remarks public, in such terms as it sees fit.

[577] The legislative history emphasizes that, to formulate its remarks, the FSMA must, in so far as they are founded, base them on the complaints it has received from the holders of the remaining securities of the offeree company. However, if these holders of securities keep their silence, this does not prevent the FSMA from making remarks on the bid if it deems them justified.

[578] In addition, section 11 of the royal decree on squeeze-outs stresses that, if the FSMA has made remarks against the bid as presented, the offeror has a period of fifteen working days from notification of these remarks to reply and, if appropriate, amend its bid to the best advantage of the holders of securities. At the end of the period of fifteen working days, the FSMA can require the offeror to take measures to safeguard the interests of the holders of securities.

[579] As indicated in the legislative history, it should finally be pointed out that it is not necessary for the FSMA to notify these complaints verbatim to the offeror, the offeree company or the market maker concerned. However, there is nothing stopping the relevant holders of securities themselves making their remarks known to those parties.

(7) Prospectus

[580] Each squeeze-out requires prior publication of a prospectus by the offeror, which must contain all the information listed in the schedule appended to the royal decree on squeeze-outs.

[581] In addition, section 12 of the decree on squeeze-outs states that, until such time as any order issued by the FSMA further to a negative opinion on its part as to whether the price offered is such as to safeguard the interests of the holders of securities of the offeree company has been heeded, it will not give any pronouncement on approval of the prospectus. In such a case, the period laid down for approval of the prospectus is suspended.

(8) Reply Memorandum

[582] Within five days from the approval of the prospectus, the board of directors of the offeree company must prepare a draft memorandum commenting on the conditions of the offer and on the statements contained in the prospectus, and must submit it to the approval of the FSMA.

[583] In this document, the board must issue a statement on whether the price offered safeguards the interests of the holders of securities and give an assessment of the independent expert's report.

(9) Period for Acceptance and Closure of the Bid

[584] The period for accepting the bid can be no less than two weeks nor more than ten weeks. This period starts running after approval of the offeree company's reply memorandum by the FSMA.

[585] Securities not presented to the offeror by expiry of the bid will nevertheless be deemed transferred to the offeror ipso iure. The funds necessary for payment of the securities thus transferred are deposited with the national depositary institution for the benefit of their former owners.

Procedural Rules Applicable to Squeeze-Outs in Private Companies

[586] The procedure for a takeover bid for the shares of a private company on the basis of section 513(2), second paragraph of the Companies Code, is provided for in the Royal Decree of 30 January 2001 implementing the Companies Code.

General Provisions

[587] Although the Royal Decree of 30 January 2001 implementing the Companies Code transposes to private companies the majority of the rules applicable to companies making or having made public offers to investors, it does not make provision for any intervention by the FSMA. The absence of any intervention by the FSMA is doubtlessly explained by the ability accorded to minority shareholders to express their comments to the offeror.

[588] The general conditions set forth in sections 210, 211, 212 and 213 of the Royal Decree of 30 January 2001 may be summarized as follows:

- the offeror must undertake to carry the offer through to its conclusion;
- the entire funds necessary for carrying through the offer have to be available;
- the offeror has to hold 95% of the voting rights and must determine the price;
- a detailed written report has to be drawn up by the offeror;
- a special report has to be drawn up by an independent auditor or accountant on the valuation method presented by the offeror and whether or not the price offered, in the auditor's or accountant's view, safeguards the interests

of the shareholders; this special report must be annexed to the report drawn up by the offeror;

- an opinion of the board of directors of the offeree, on the special report of the independent auditor or accountant company has to be prepared commenting on the aforementioned report of the offeror, on the special report of the independent auditor or accountant and on whether or not, in its view, the price offered safeguards the interests of the shareholders.

Publicizing the Procedure

[589] Where not all the shares are in registered form, a notice indicating the place where the shareholders can obtain the aforementioned reports has to be published twice at an interval of at least eight days in a press publication with national circulation and in a press publication in the region in which the offeree company has its registered office. Where all the shares are in registered form, these reports have to be sent to the shareholders by recorded delivery.

Remarks by the Shareholders

[590] The shareholders have a period of thirty working days as from the date of publication of the second notice referred to above or as from the date of dispatch of the recorded delivery letters in which to intimate their grievances with regard to the offer. If grievances are made, the offeror can uphold its offer or alter it so that it is more favourable to the shareholders. In any event, the offeror gives notice of whether it is upholding or altering its offer. Where bearer certificates have been issued, the notice is published in the press or, where all shares are in registered form, the notice is sent to the shareholders by recorded delivery.

Closure of the Offer

[591] With the exception of shares whose owners have, prior to closure of the offer, intimated in writing to the offeror that they refuse to dispose of their shares, the shares not presented to the offeror are transferred automatically to the offeror.

[592] Payment for the shares is made no later than one month after closure of the offer.

[593] The funds necessary for payment of the shares transferred are deposited ipso iure with the national depository institution for the account of the former owners.

BUY-BACK OF OWN SHARES

Introduction

[594] The buy-back of own shares is an operation by which a company acquires its own shares by way of purchase or exchange. In spite of the risks that such an operation can entail, it has progressively been accepted by lawmakers, provided certain conditions are adhered to. Indeed, redemption by a company of its own shares can prove useful in a number of respects. *Inter alia,* it enables the company:

- to regulate the stock market price of its securities in the case of an abnormal drop due to false rumours,
- to produce an 'accretive effect' on the securities and hence increase the proportional holdings of the shareholders,
- to forearm against a hostile takeover, to reclassify its securities; and
- to carry out certain reorganizational measures.

[595] The coming into force of Directive 2006/68/EC of the European Parliament and of the Council of 6 September 2006 amending Council Directive 77/91/EEC has slightly amended the existing rules. The Royal Decree of 8 October 2008, which implemented this directive in Belgian law, came into force on 1 January 2009 (the 'Royal Decree') and was confirmed in a legislative vote on 6 May 2009.

Conditions for a Buy-Back of Own Shares

Decision by the General Meeting

[596] The general meeting of shareholders must authorize the board of directors to resolve to buy back shares of the company. This authorization must be approved in accordance with the quorums and majorities laid down for amendments to the company's objects. Since the buy-back decision lies exclusively with the board of directors, it constitutes a power unique to it and therefore must comply with the rules set down in section 523 of the Companies Code in relation to conflicts of interests. However, this prior authorization is not required if the securities are allotted to members of the workforce or where the articles of association authorize the board of directors to buy the company's shares back in order to avoid it suffering serious, imminent harm.

[597] Under the old rules, the maximum validity for the authorization conferred by the general meeting of shareholders was eighteen months. The special power conferred on the board of directors to acquire own shares to avert serious, imminent harm was valid for three years. The first change made by the Royal Decree of 8 October 2008 is to increase the validity of the basic authorization issued by the general meeting to the board of directors to five years. The validity of the special power to allow the board of directors to resolve to acquire own shares to avert serious, imminent harm remains unchanged.

Underlying Conditions

[598] Under the old rule, to be able to buy back its own shares, the company could not be in a position to hold shares representing over 10% of its subscribed capital at the same time. To assess this ceiling, the shares already held by the company at the time of the buy-back were to be taken into consideration. The second change made by the Royal Decree is to raise this maximum threshold of 10% of the value of the own shares that a company can acquire. Now, the par value, failing which the accounting value of the shares or profit-sharing certificates acquired by the company, or of the shares or profit-sharing certificates to which the other certificates relate, may not exceed 20% of the subscribed capital. We would point out that, as regards cross-holdings, the ceiling has not be changed and remains at 10%. The resultant situation is somewhat paradoxical.

[599] In addition, the buy-back must be financed using distributable profits within the meaning of section 617 of the Companies Code.

[600] A third change concerns calculation of the distributable profits that a company must have to be able to buy back its own shares. Section 620 of the Companies Code now states that this calculation has to be done by adding to the sums directly affected by an acquisition of own shares, the amount provided for shares previously acquired by the company and that it has in its portfolio, together with shares acquired by a person acting as a nominee for the company in question.

[601] The operation may only relate to fully paid-up shares and therefore cannot be used as a means of releasing the shareholders from having to paying up their calls.

[602] Finally, regardless of what form the bid takes, it has to be addressed to all of the shareholders, and under the same terms. This latter condition is not, however, required where the redemption of own shares was authorized by a general meeting deciding unanimously and at which all the shareholders were present or represented or where the redemption takes place on a stock market (section 620(1), (5°) of the Companies Code as amended by the Act of 20 July 2006). In these cases, the company could redeem its shares under private sales, i.e., with one or more shareholders under differing terms.

Exceptions

[603] Section 621 of the Companies Code sets forth a certain number of situations in which the decision to buy back own shares need not either be subject to prior authorization of the general meeting or fulfil the conditions set out in the previous point. This includes the situation where shares have been acquired with a view to their being immediately retired or those acquired following a universal transfer of assets. This latter exception is aimed at universal transfers resulting from a reverse merger, i.e., a merger involving absorption by a subsidiary of its parent company.

Form

[604] Excepting the cases analysed above in which the own shares can be bought back by way of private sales or via the stock exchange, the company may only carry out such an operation by way of an offer made under the same conditions to all the shareholders of the company. If the offer qualifies as a public offer under the Takeover Bids Act, it must comply with all the rules set out in the preceding chapter.

Buy-Back of Own Shares by Listed Companies

[605] As already briefly stated above, section 620(1), first paragraph (5°), states that:

> the acquisition offer must be made under the same conditions to all the shareholders and, as the case may be, to all holders of profit-sharing certificates or holders of other certificates, . . .; likewise, listed companies and those whose shares are admitted to trading on a non-regulated market organised in a daily manner by a market maker may purchase their own shares or their certificates on these markets without an acquisition offer having to be made to the shareholders or holders of certificates, provided that they guarantee the equality of treatment of the shareholders or holders of certificates that are in the same conditions, by equivalence of the offered price.

[606] At first sight, a buy-back of shares on a regulated market seems to abide by the principle of equality to the extent that all the shareholders in the general public can become sellers. However, if demand outstrips supply, the first to reply will prevail over the others, without any due reduction being able to be effected. In this regard, the FSMA considers that equality of treatment is not to be assessed in terms of access to share-acquisition transactions. It is therefore necessary to determine the conditions for application of this provision in light of the principle of equality as thus construed.

[607] In its opinion of 14 April 2005, the CBFA had occasion to analyse the various techniques for stock market acquisition recognized by the Rule Book. The CBFA examined to what extent such operations ensured equality of treatment and could therefore be exempted from the obligation to address the offer to all of the shareholders. It took the view that share-purchase transactions effected in the central order book comply with the equality of treatment principle but such was not necessarily the case with cross-orders, even if they were transacted via the central order book. The reason for this was that they entail the simultaneous production and execution at the same price by a single member of the market of two opposing client orders for the same quantity of given securities. Because they are not subject to the generalized face-off between supply and demand, the operation thus results in inequality as regards price.

[608] The Royal Decree also extends the scope of the exception to the obligation on a company to address the same buy-back offer to all its shareholders. The Royal Decree replaces this exception with the following rules: listed companies and companies whose securities are admitted to trading on a 'MTF' may, in so far as the MTF functions on the basis of daily trading and a central order book, purchase their own shares or certificates without a takeover offer having to be sent to the shareholders or holders of certificates on condition that they guarantee equality of treatment of shareholders or holders of certificates under like conditions, provided the price offered is the same.

INSIDER TRADING

Introduction

[609] The offence of insider trading is a notion of criminal law in which an investor utilizes privileged information relating to a listed company. The insider exploits the period between the time at which the information comes into his possession and that when the information is known publicly to carry out his transactions. Prosecution of insider trading is therefore intended to penalize the usurping of equality that could arise on a market and to maintain investors' confidence by assuring them that they will not be systematically disadvantaged by comparison with professional investors.

[610] With this in mind, the Act of 2 August 2002 on regulation of the financial sector contains a set of rules aimed at proscribing certain behaviour by persons in possession of privileged information. The insider trading rules contained in the old sections 181-191 of the Act of 4 December 1990 have been incorporated into section 25 of the Act of 2 August 2002. The rules set down in section 25 of the Act are nonetheless far broader in scope than the old rules. Before dealing in more detail with behaviour the act proscribes, it is appropriate to define the notion of privileged information.

Privileged Information

[611] Section 2(14°) of the Act of 2 August 2002 defines the notion of 'privileged information' as follows:

> any information that has not been made public, that is of a precise nature and that, directly or indirectly, concerns one or more issuers of financial instruments or one or more financial instruments and that, were it rendered public, would be likely materially to affect the price of the financial instruments concerned or that of derivative financial instruments linked thereto.

[612] The same definition is incumbent on those whose task it is to execute orders concerning financial instruments. For instruments derived from basic products, 'privileged information' nevertheless has to be interpreted as any information that has not been rendered public, that is of a precise nature and that directly or indirectly concerns one or more such derivative instruments and that users of the markets on which these instruments are traded would expect to receive in accordance with normal practice on those markets.

[613] Information is considered as 'likely materially to affect the price of the financial instruments concerned or that of derivative financial instruments linked thereto' where a reasonable investor would be liable to use the information as forming part of the bases on which he makes his investment decisions.

[614] The information is deemed to be '*precise in nature*' if it makes mention of a set of circumstances that exist or will exist and if it is sufficiently precise that one can consider that that set of circumstances could have effects on the prices of the financial instruments concerned or of derivative financial instruments linked to them.

[615] In short, to be privileged, the information must be sufficiently precise, must not have been rendered public and must be likely materially to affect the price. The privileged information may nevertheless still be incomplete, stem from a simple rumour or only have been made public to a selection of the potential investors. In reality, everything turns on an interpretation of the facts. Moreover, privileged information concerns both issuers of financial instruments and the financial instruments themselves and instruments linked thereto.

Extent of the Prohibition

[616] Section 25 of the Act of 2 August 2002 prohibits all persons:

1. possessing information they know or ought to know is privileged in nature:
   (i) on their own behalf or on behalf of third parties, from directly or indirectly acquiring or disposing of, or attempting to acquire or dispose of, the financial instruments to which the information pertains except in the case of transactions carried out to ensure execution of an obligation to acquire or dispose of financial instruments where that obligation has become enforceable and results from an agreement contracted before the party in question came into possession of the privileged information in question;
   (ii) from disclosing such information to any other person, other than in the normal course of his work, profession or duties;
   (iii) from, on the basis of the privileged information, recommending to a third party that he acquire or dispose of, or procure the acquisition or disposal by another person of, the financial instruments to which the information pertains.
2. from carrying out transactions or placing orders:
   (i) that give or are likely to give false or misleading indications of the supply, demand or price of or for one or more financial instruments; or
   (ii) that, through the action of one or more persons acting in concert, fix the price of one or more financial instruments at an abnormal or artificial level, unless the person carrying out the transactions or placing the orders proves that the reasons inducing him to do so are legitimate and that the transactions or orders in question are in conformity with market practices accepted on the market concerned.
3. from carrying out transactions or placing orders that make recourse to fictitious procedures or any other form of deception or ploy;
4. from spreading information or rumours, through the intervention of the media, via the internet or by any other means, that give or are likely to give false or misleading indications relating to financial instruments where he knew or ought to have known that the information was false or misleading. In the case of journalists acting within the course of their profession, such spreading of information must be evaluated in light of the rules applying to their profession unless such persons directly or indirectly draw a benefit or profit from the spreading of the information in question;

5. from committing other acts defined on the advice of the FSMA that hinder or disrupt or are likely to hinder or disrupt the proper functioning, integrity and transparency of the market;
6. from taking part in any attempt to commit the acts referred to in the first five above paragraphs;
7. from inciting any other person or persons to commit acts that, if he were to commit them himself, would be proscribed pursuant the first five paragraphs.

[617] However, none of these prohibitions applies:

- to operations carried out for reasons having to do with monetary policy, foreign exchange policy or the management of public debt by a Member State of the European Economic Area, the European System of Central Banks, the National Bank of Belgium or any other central bank of another Member State of the European Economic Area, the Securities Regulation Fund, [. . .], the communities, regions, French Community Commission, the provinces, municipalities, conurbations and local authority federations or by any other person acting on behalf of any of the foregoing;
- to operations involving own shares carried out in the framework of 'buy-back' programmes, or to measures to stabilize a financial instrument, subject to such operations being carried out in accordance with Regulation no. 2273/2003 of 22 December 2003 implementing Directive 2003/6/EC of the European Parliament and of the Council as regards exemptions for buy-back programmes and stabilization of financial instruments.

[618] All of these prohibitions apply to the acts referred to in so far as they concern:

- financial instruments that are admitted to trading on a Belgian regulated market or any other market or alternative trading facility, or that form the object of an application for admission to trading on such a market or facility. These prohibitions apply equally regardless of whether the acts in question are carried out in Belgium or abroad, whether the transactions in question are executed on the market concerned or outside that market;
- financial instruments that are admitted to trading on a foreign regulated market or any other market or alternative trading facility organized abroad and designated by the Royal Decree on the advice of the FSMA, or that form the object of an application for admission to trading on such a market or facility, provided the acts in question are carried out in Belgium, whether the transactions in question are executed on the market concerned or outside that market;

8. financial instruments that are not admitted to trading on the markets or alternative trading facilities referred to above but whose value is dependent on a financial instrument referred to above.

[619] This provision also states that, in the context of a company or other legal person, all these prohibitions also apply to natural persons participating in the decision to carry out a transaction or place an order on behalf of the legal person in question.

[620] Section 25 of the Act of 2 August 2002 also prohibits all persons:

- from disseminating information or rumours, through the media, Internet or any other means, which give or are likely to give false or misleading indications on the situation, more particularly the financial situation, of a credit institution, an insurance company, an investments company or settlement institution or similar, likely to affect its financial stability while she knew or should have known that the information were false or misleading;
- from providing false or misleading information or data or from performing any other act constituting a manipulation of the calculation of the reference index.

Powers of the FSMA

[621] The FSMA has power to oversee application of section 25 of the Act of 2 August 2002 relating to insider trading and, to this end, has the powers of investigation set forth in sections 34 and 35 of the Act of 2 August 2002.

[622] Apart from the criminal penalties to which anyone breaching the above rules is liable, the FSMA has power to take administrative measures against offenders. It can order any natural or legal person to heed the provisions of section 25 of the Act of 2 August 2002, make its decision public and make it subject to coercive penalties. It also has power to impose administrative fines on offenders.

Made in the USA
Monee, IL
18 October 2026

66037593R10085